M000158648

#THEPOWEROFJOY

THE POWER OF JOY

A STRAIGHT UP GUIDE TO LASTING FREEDOM, EFFORTLESS ABUNDANCE, AND A LIMITLESS LIFE

NICK BREAU

Copyright © 2016 by Nick Breau

All rights reserved. This book or any portion there of may not be reproduced or used in any manner whatsoever without the express written permission of the publisher except for the use of brief quotations in a book review.

Printed in the United States of America

First Printing, 2016

ISBN 978-1-941142-80-6

Nick Breau

www.discoverthepowerofjoy.com

THE MOST IMPORTANT DECISION WE
MAKE IS WHETHER WE
BELIEVE WE LIVE IN A FRIENDLY OR A
HOSTILE UNIVERSE.

—ALBERT EINSTEIN

TABLE OF CONTENTS

INTRODUCTION

FOR THE FIRST THIRTY years of my life, I operated on autopilot. I followed the navigation plan everyone in society believes they must follow in order to be happy. I sought financial stability by obtaining a bachelor's degree in computer science and working in the technology sector. I fell in love, got married, and later had two amazing kids, a son and daughter. Becoming a father and watching my little ones grow, laugh, play, and cry have been the most cherished experiences of my life.

I was happy, for the most part. Like the majority of people, I experienced the usual ups and downs of life. I had great friends and neighbours and lived a relatively stress-free life. Yet deep down, I always felt like something was missing.

Of the 52 weeks in a year, I only had three weeks' paid vacation. Most of my life was spent in a cubical, under fluorescent lighting, with eyes glazed over from too much time in front of a screen. I had achieved exactly what I had set out to achieve, exactly what society told me I should seek out, and yet there was a niggling feeling that something wasn't right.

This "perfect" life I had been taught to desire was starting to feel more and more out of place. Some days, I literally felt like a caged animal, existing solely so that I could work to pay the bills. Surely, I hadn't chosen to be born into this earthly existence to live such a mediocre life?

Everywhere I looked, everyone was doing the same thing—putting work first, with joy, fun, and freedom a distant second—but deep inside me, something was screaming that there had to be more.

While solving complex computer problems was my day job, personal development and spirituality became my passion. I spent years reading books by top authors, acquiring training in dozens of alternative healing methods, and paying big bucks to hire top coaches from all over the world in order to expand my inner awareness. I studied topics such as holographic universe theory, the law of attraction, human behaviour and consciousness. Like a sponge, I spent years soaking in everything I could.

I hacked computers for a living, but now, I wanted to hack something different. I wanted to hack my life. My reality. My human experience. I wanted to find a better way to experience the life I was living, and I knew it was out there.

I believed what I needed to find was deep, and that in order to discover something so deep and highly transformative it would have to be complex and hard to find. Boy, was I wrong.

One day, something clicked. I figured it out. I experienced a shift. A big one. But it had nothing to do with discovering a complicated methodology. And it wasn't something I found by analyzing a 400-page book or achieving deep states of consciousness through hours of meditation. Nor did I find it by creating vision boards or reciting affirmations. What I found was sitting right under my nose, and it was easily accessible to anyone, at any time.

I shifted so profoundly as a result of this realization, that it transformed my entire outer reality. I used it to manifest my biggest desires, and I used it to create the life I truly wanted, the life my soul was aching for.

In a short period of time, my net worth rocketed to over seven figures, thanks to the sale of a company with which I had been employed. I ended up leaving my marriage to later find myself in the most incredible, synchronistic, twin-soul relationship with an incredibly beautiful, big-hearted woman. I found myself living on the beach and loving every minute of my life.

In short, I began to live the life that I had always hoped was possible. The life that the incessant, nagging feeling my cubicle time inspired me to seek out.

Since then life has become truly magical. No more effort and struggle just to get by. With this secret ingredient, things fall into place effortlessly, with absolute ease.

Sound too good to be true?

In the pages that follow, I'll share both my personal experience and the road map I followed, including easy and powerful techniques that I'm hoping you will try. The information contained in this book is not just abstract knowledge, it's a comprehensive guide designed with hands-on tools to help you shift any aspect of your life. It's a formula I wish someone could have shared with me a long time ago. This formula that has changed my life, as well as the lives of my clients, and I know this formula will bring the same kind of joy, ease, and abundance into your life – a life where you're not just settling for the circumstances in your reality, you're defining them to be exactly what you desire.

PART 1

WELCOME TO THE NEW REALITY

Discover the Life You're Meant to Live

WELCOME TO THE NEW REALITY

IF THERE IS ONE thing I know for certain about life, it's that change is the only constant.

Some days our lives play out just as we expect it. Other days, we experience events so overwhelming the wind gets knocked right out of us. Events that not only change the course of our lives but that also change the way we experience our entire reality.

For me, one such event happened late in the summer of 2012.

I was living in a small, rundown, ocean-side cottage I had purchased a number of years prior and was spending most of my time meditating and reflecting on life. It was the first time in my life when I felt really alone and also the first time my focus was solely on me.

A few months before, I had made a decision that significantly altered the course of my life. I did something that most of society frowns upon - I left my marriage.

Even though I had no doubt, in either my mind or my heart, that I had made the right decision, I was struggling. I greatly missed being able to see and hug my kids every day, and was now only spending half the week with them. I was living two hours away from my friends, and from my immediate family. Fears around access to my kids, where I would go, and what I would do next continually crept in. All the things that used to feel stable had been left behind with my decision to leave. The familiarity of the home I had left behind, the neighbours and friends I went to for support, and my full-time job, all were gone. I was at an all time low.

In my despair, as I was weeding the vegetable garden one morning, I did something I had been doing on occasion in recent years. I asked the universe to show me a sign that everything was going to be ok.

A few hours later I was dressed, showered, and getting ready to run into town to pick up a few things. As I approached my car a strong intuitive nudge, which I usually receive as a feeling in my gut, urged me to take an alternative route to my usual coastal drive. This strong feeling was crying out for me to take the highway. As I much prefer the beauty of my usual coastal drive, I carried on, ignoring the message. As I got closer and closer to the fork in the road where I needed to decide which route to take, the voice got louder. It persisted, and I gave in.

I turned right, and headed down the highway ramp. Checking quickly over my left shoulder I easily merged into the traffic of the busy highway, with a large truck behind me and a mid-size car up ahead. I noticed the car in front had a custom licence plate. It read "TRSTGOD." Trust God. The request I had made earlier in the day while seeking comfort and reassurance, immediately rushed into my mind. I was left in complete awe at the spectacular response of the universe. The message couldn't have been more clear.

From this point forward, everything changed. If God, the universe, my inner being, or who or whatever was in control had the power to create and deliver this message, who was I to doubt what was possible? Who was I to doubt my decision to separate from my wife, or any other event in my life, for that matter? If any event in my life up to this point has had a profound, knock-the-wind-right-out-of-me kind of impact, this was it. Although I had been studying concepts such as consciousness, spirituality and the nature of reality for a long time, this was truly a defining moment, completely shifting the way I perceived my reality forever. This was the moment when everything changed.

From this point forward, I totally let go. I relaxed into my experience and trusted. Not only was I changing but so was the very reality that surrounded me.

A number of months later, I met my current partner of three years, Anik. Although the connection wasn't obvious at first, it quickly became very apparent as we continued to spend time together. We soon realized that the connection we shared was different than anything either of us had experienced. Not only did we share a mutual attraction, but also several incredible synchronicities: we had almost identical names (both of us being called "Nick" by our respective parents), we both drove (and still drive) the exact same vehicle, and to top it all off, we realized that we both ended up leaving our marriages on the exact same day, long before we ever met!

Over the last few years, my life has continued to shift in positive and amazing ways. I've built a beautiful house where the cottage once stood. My relationship with my kids is amazing and the time we spend together here at the beach is nothing short of magical. I continue to experience incredible synchronicities, many of which I share in this book. Every day, I am filled with appreciation for the experiences in my life. I am grateful for seeing the beauty of what is truly possible for each and every person, and for knowing that this same beauty and magic is available to everyone on this planet.

It's this same beauty and magic that I'm hoping, through the teachings of this book, will present itself to you.

DESIRE MISUNDERSTOOD

ONE MORNING, WHILE DRIVING into work, I had one of the most significant personal realizations of my life. At that time in my life I was reading books by Eckhart Tolle and Wayne Dyer. I was studying the law of attraction and meditating on almost a daily basis. But these weren't the sources of this great realization. My profound realization came to me in the form of a song that the Spice Girls had recorded nearly a decade earlier.

The main chorus of this song goes like this:

"Yo, I'll tell you what I want, what I really really want,
So tell me what you want, what you really really want,
I'll tell you what I want, what I really really want,
So tell me what you want, what you really really want,
I wanna, I wanna, I wanna, I wanna, I wanna really really
really wanna zigazig ha."

This got me thinking. What is it that **I** really really want? And not just what do I really want, but why? What is the driving force behind my desires? Why does anyone want the things they want? Are our desires encoded into our DNA or is there more to it than this?

Even as a child, I had an analytical mind; internally dissecting the world around me, wondering why, at a deeper level, things were the way they were. As I asked these questions around desire my mind immediately began its analysis. The answers I found sent me down a spiralling adventure, which would ultimately transform my entire reality. It's the seed that eventually led to the birth of this book, and, it brings me to the realization that I should be thanking the Spice Girls in my acknowledgments!

I'd like to ask you a question. Take a few minutes to think about it. What are your biggest desires and what would change if you were actually living those desires?

The sentence you used to answer that question most likely started with the words "I would feel." If it's not apparent, try asking yourself that question in a different way. What would you gain by realizing that big desire?

What I realized that day is that all desires are rooted in feelings. The reason we want or do anything, is that we believe that having those things, or taking those actions, will make us feel better in some way. We believe that having more money will bring more freedom and relief. We believe that being in a relationship will make us feel more loved. We believe that owning that bigger house or fancier car will make us more fulfilled.

Every single decision we make, every action we take, and every desire we seek is founded on the belief that it will bring improvement in the way we feel. Everything we have ever done or ever will do is with the hope that it will kick up our how-good- do-I-feel-o-meter a notch or two.

At the surface we all seem to want different things. Some people want to raise a family. Some want to run a Fortune 500 company. Others want to sail the world or become a movie star. However, deep down, everyone is really just looking for the same thing. We all want to be happy.

Looking for Happiness in All the Wrong Places

I'll never forget my daughter's first day of Grade 1. Anyone who's spent time with my daughter knows that inside that tall, slim, blonde-haired, six-year-old is a strong-willed little girl who doesn't like to be told what to do. Not being overly excited about starting school, she was filled with nerves and plenty of tears as she marched (or maybe it was more like got carried) to the car.

As we drove to the school, I started thinking about all the subjects she may learn, not only in first grade, but also throughout her entire education. Math, science, history, reading and writing. Like being hit by a ton of bricks I also realized that although these are important topics that will most certainly help her throughout the course of her life, at no point in her formal education would she ever be taught the one thing that would bring her the most success of all:

How to be happy.

We all know what happiness is. We've all experienced both the highs and the lows of life and the various emotional states that go along with it. But at no point were we ever really taught how to be happy.

I want you to ask yourself another question. Before you move on to the next paragraph I want you to come up with one word. I want you to ask yourself what your number one priority has been for the last three months, six months and twelve months. What one word would you associate to each of these periods of time?

Work? School? Making more money? Taking care of the kids? Getting ready for a triathlon?

What about being happy?

In recent speaking engagements I've enjoyed putting my audience on the spot by asking them this very question. I ask each audience member to come up with one word representing his or her number one priority. I then ask for a show of hands for those who chose work, those who chose school, and those who chose taking care of their kids.

And then, I ask for a show of hands from those whose number one priority it is to be happy.

Often I don't see any hands raised in response to that question, and the overall average of those who do raise their hands would be around 2% - A mere two percent of the entire audience actively making happiness a priority!

Now, for a follow up question. If you could measure your level of happiness on a scale of 0 to 10, 0 being not a single smile in the last 6 months and 10 being that if you were any happier your head would pop off, where would you rank yourself?

When asking this question of an audience, I've never seen a 10, or even a 9. A few hands start to appear around 8 with the numbers beginning to grow at 7, 6 and 5. Based on my experience over the last six months, most individuals are averaging somewhere between a 4 and a 6 on the happiness scale.

Take some time and think about where you sit on that scale. Where do you sit today? Last week? Last month? Last year? At what point in your life were you the happiest, and where did that joy go?

Final question: Do you believe happiness is an inside job, or do you believe happiness is something you need to seek out and find through achievement?

When asking this final question of my audience not a single person has gotten this question wrong. Everyone asked knows that joy and happiness is an inside job.

But if happiness is an inside job, why are people ranking so low on the happiness scale? Why aren't we seeing many 8's, 9's or 10's? Why are most people only about half as happy as they have the potential to be?

Your inner state of being and where you sit at an emotional level isn't black and white and can't be defined by a mathematical equation. What I can tell you from my own experience, and what I believe to be true for most of society, is that people tend to look for happiness in all the wrong places.

I remember being told at a young age how I needed to live my life. The messages were that school was important and that I needed to get good grades and move on to university to earn a bachelor's degree. Also, that if I wanted to be happy, I needed to be successful and make lots of money.

I played this all out perfectly. I got good grades, and upon graduation I landed a job in a junior position at a tech company and of course, I proved myself by working my way up the corporate ladder. With every goal I achieved, with every advancement I made, a new goal would quickly replace the old one. If I was in a junior developer position, I needed to work hard to become intermediate. Once I was intermediate, I couldn't be happy until I was senior. Once I achieved a senior position, I needed more. Wherever I sat, never felt good enough, as a new desire would always appear on the horizon and the familiar feelings of being unaccomplished would begin to settle in.

No matter what level I had achieved in any given moment, I believed it was never good enough. There was always something bigger to be achieved, something more to be had, something my ego was telling me had to be accomplished if I wanted to be happy.

At the surface we're all chasing goals. We want the better job. More money. A bigger house. We want all of these things because we believe they will make us happy. In reality, we're just like dogs chasing our own tails as we search for the one thing, the one achievement that will finally bring us lifelong happiness.

The truth? That 'one thing' does not (and never will) exist. You will always want more. If you really want to be happy - and I know you do - you need to redirect your focus from the things you believe will make you happy, to the actual state of happiness itself.

You need to learn to be happy right here, right now. Proactively taking charge of the way you feel won't only shift your inner state of being, it will change the way you experience your entire reality.

A Lesson in Doing Laundry

I recently spent an evening with a few friends at our beach house. Discussions with friends always seem to spiral into topics like the meaning of life, consciousness, and the effects of our mental and emotional states. This day was no different.

Frank, whom I had just met a month prior, was asking about my client work and how I help people break free from struggles and achieve higher states of joy. Little did I know, he was about to provide me with the perfect example of why so many people are unable to maintain a consistent level of happiness.

At one point I was explaining to Frank that most people have very little emotional awareness. That very few people spend time reflecting on how they feel or why they feel the way they do. I asked Frank how he had felt most of that day. His response? Angry.

I then asked Frank how he felt when he woke up that morning. He proceeded to tell me he actually had an amazing morning. He woke up happy, with a little time to play guitar before work, and he enjoyed a satisfying breakfast.

I then asked him when it was that he lost the happiness and switched to anger.

After a few seconds of thought, Frank began to laugh and gave me a look of total amazement. His answer? "When I noticed I had three loads of laundry to fold!" Frank explained to me how folding laundry was one of this most hated chores and that on his way out the door, he had noticed that he had three loads of laundry waiting to be folded and put away once he got home. Not only did Frank's hatred for folding laundry trigger his immediate shift from a state of joy to a state of anger, but then, because he allowed this anger to stick around, he also ended up feeling lousy and short-tempered for the rest of the day. He had allowed something as simple as a few loads of laundry to ruin his entire day.

Frank's situation perfectly exemplifies a common problem. Most of us unknowingly give away our control over how we feel to the circumstances that surround us. We become emotionally destabilized by forfeiting our emotional power to circumstances beyond our control.

On any given day, we experience a number of circumstances. Although we'd like to think we know how our day will play out, it isn't always the case. On occasion your vehicle may decide to break down. Your partners may decide to end your relationship. The co-worker in the office down the hall may get a promotion while you don't.

Such circumstances can be an unpleasant part of the human experience. The problem, however, isn't the circumstances. It's how we allow these situations to dictate the way we feel. If I get a raise and my co-worker doesn't, then I get happy and he gets angry or sad. If the roles are reversed, I'm the angry one. Because I have no control over the circumstance, and I allow the circumstance to control my emotional state, I thus forfeit my control over the way I feel.

In the previous section I've explained how it doesn't serve you to focus on the stuff you believe will make you happy. Instead you are far better served by focusing on the direct route of simply being happy. Reclaiming control over the way you feel by detaching your emotional state from your circumstances is the very first step. This can be done by making the conscious decision, the moment you wake up, that you will be happy today regardless of what's currently happening in your life or of any unexpected surprises that might occur. When discussing this with my clients, I tell them they want to be "Fuck It Happy." That no matter what is going on in any given moment, regardless of how painstaking a situation might be, it is possible to say "fuck it" and choose to be happy anyway.

Before moving on to the next section, I suggest taking some time to reflect on your emotional state of being. When you find yourself in an unhappy place, are you able to determine the outer world circumstances responsible for removing you from a happier state of being? Are they small and less obvious factors such as folding laundry or not receiving a phone call from a friend? Or, are they more obvious situations such as a relationship that fell apart or an unwanted employment situation. Are you able to let go of those circumstances and reclaim your power?

YOUR INNER BEING HAS AN INBOX

HOPEFULLY, YOU CAN REMEMBER at least one time in your life where you were predominantly happy. For many, that time was childhood. What happens to pull us away from this state of joy? Some people can easily identify what caused happiness to end, but others may feel as though that happy place is long gone with no rhyme or reason. If you feel like you've lost your happiness, or most of it, have you ever wondered where it went?

The births of my children were some of the happiest moments of my life. Watching my son and daughter grow has been truly life changing. I've spent hours wondering why it is so easy for them to be happy. Why is it that almost every morning they wake up grinning ear to ear, excited for the day ahead? My son, approaching the age of four, will randomly turn to me throughout the day, exclaiming "I love you, Daddy," as we're putting together a puzzle or having lunch. My daughter, now six, never questions her experience or rationalizes her decisions. She does whatever feels best for her without a care in the world. She does whatever she can to follow her flow, not allowing anyone (including Mommy or Daddy) to take her out of it without a fight.

What happens to us between then and now? Why is it that at a young age we are in such a loving state, almost unconditionally happy yet as adults getting out of bed happy often seems like a challenge, and we feel like batteries that have lost their charge?

We've established that the decisions you make and the actions you take are rooted in your desire to feel better. Those desires are driven by your emotions, which are an integral part of the human experience. You may not realize that emotions have an important purpose on many levels. Understanding emotions and how they impact your life is fundamental to learning how to shift your human experience.

For most people feelings are a by-product of the circumstances of their lives, but you give your power away by allowing circumstances to dictate your emotions. This may be the way you may have operated your entire life. Later in this book, I'll teach you techniques to help you gain better control of your emotions and reclaim your power. But first, I want you to understand the true source of the way you feel.

If you were to stack the range of available emotions from the least to the most pleasurable, powerless would be found at the bottom and joy would sit at the top. Joy is, in all likelihood, the most sought after emotion. Coincidentally, it's also the most naturally occurring emotion. It's what sits at the core of your being. Joy is what you are. Whether you can feel it or not, it's always present deep inside of you. It's your natural state of being.

Back to kids for a minute and the fact that finding their happy place takes little or no effort. In fact, it's automatic. Why?

Because at such a young age they still exist in a more pure state of being. They have not yet allowed their ego to begin to create fears and judgments. They have not yet experienced major traumas that cause them to repress emotions that cover up this natural state. They have not yet formed beliefs that prevent them from allowing their joy to shine.

At birth your inner state of being exists in its purest form. You are free from negative programming placed upon you by your surroundings. Your connection to your higher self, your soul, your inner being, is strong. You grow older and live the full buffet of experiences that life brings to your table. You start to shape beliefs. You experience emotions, both pleasant and unpleasant. Unknowingly, you begin to repress unpleasant emotions that result from the negative experiences and traumas in your life. Over time, these emotions may disappear from your conscious awareness. Internally, however, like ignored messages in an email inbox, the unprocessed emotions remain.

Life goes on, and as you focus on current events, those negative emotions, which you have not fully processed, are buried in your subconscious. As they continue to pile up, they slowly start to cover up that state of joy. You are likely unaware this is going on. Over time, as you continue to collect negative emotional baggage, your state of joy gets pushed beneath layers of repressed negative emotions.

The end result? Joy is no longer natural and easily experienced. Your dominant emotion of joy has shifted and been covered up by something else.

You were born perfect. Take a moment to allow that thought to sink in. The moment you were born you were nothing less than perfect. Any parent who has held their newborn in their arms knows this is fact. Love and joy are as natural to you as eating and breathing. It is what you are. It is important for you to realize you still embody that perfection. You are still whole. You are the exact same creature that came through the birth canal years ago.

You have picked up beliefs and held onto negative emotions over the course of your life. Like unwanted hitchhikers, these are the only thing between you and the knowledge of your own perfection. The only thing between your current state of being, and being in the place of joy, are emotions you've repressed and false beliefs you've collected that are robbing you of your happiness.

Your Inner Being Has an Inbox

Have you ever considered how much time you spend maintaining your email inbox? I'm a fairly organized guy in most areas of my life, but for some reason, I've always had a hard time managing and staying on top of all the emails I get over the course of a week. As of this morning I have over forty thousand emails in my inbox and have been hovering around my storage capacity for a little over a month.

I long for the days when my inbox felt organized, easy to manage, and clean. Free of spam, Facebook and Twitter notifications, and bill reminders. Now that my inbox has grown beyond a manageable size, working on it now seems like too much of a daunting undertaking to even consider. I very much regret not having taken the time to delete, archive, or categorize every single message that found its way to me back when I had my inbox under control.

Why am I talking about my inbox and poor management skills?

Because our inner beings have inboxes too. And odds are, they also needs some work.

It's an analogy I like to use to help people understand how the state of our inner being's inbox impacts our current emotional state.

At the time of your birth your inbox is empty. Clean and free of clutter, an empty inbox feels good and allows you to maintain your natural state of joy.

As your life unfolds, you experience myriad events. With each event, an email is delivered into your inbox and attached to it, are the emotions pertaining to that event. Pleasant events deliver happy emotions into your inbox and because you enjoy the contents of the message, you happily open and give your attention to it. Opening up these messages feels good and allows you to fully process these emotions.

Negative emotions, delivered through unwanted circumstances, also end up in this very same inbox. When a negative emotion is delivered you have two options. The first is to acknowledge the message. To open it and feel it. By feeling the emotion you are opening up the message and processing it. By taking the time to process these messages you delete them and let the emotions go. This is the ideal course of action. These emotions have presented themselves because they need to be felt.

Because negative emotions are unpleasant, most of us ignore these messages. Because they are left unread, they remain sitting in your inbox collecting dust. Over time the number of unread negative emotional messages grows, and as time passes, older, unread messages get pushed further down your inbox as they are consciously forgotten. Eventually, your inbox becomes overcrowded and begins to run out of space. The number of negative emotions far outweighs the positive ones, which get lost in the shuffle. That natural state of joy and the positive emotions you've been storing are lost and difficult to feel. Not only does this impact your levels of happiness and inner peace, but it also impacts your health and begins to attract a growing number of difficult circumstances in your life.

Have you ever accidentally left a carton of milk on the counter only to have your roommate throw it across the room in a fit of rage against your not putting it back in the fridge? Odds are your roommate isn't just extra sensitive to spoiled milk. His inner being inbox has accumulated a huge amount of anger over the years and is now overflowing. Because anger makes up the larger part of his inbox, it has become his dominant emotion. Until he chooses to deal with his anger by releasing the repressed emotion (thus deleting those messages) it will dominate the experiences in his life, the way he feels, and the situations he attracts. Over time it will likely have a negative impact on his physical health and well-being.

If your inner being inbox contains negative emotions, don't panic. Everyone experiences negative feelings and trauma. We all have repressed emotions. We all have (or have had) negative emotions sitting in our inbox. The good news is that every unwanted emotion sitting in your inbox isn't part of you and can be removed. Returning to a state of joy, no matter how overflowing with negative emotions your inbox may be, can be accomplished by releasing those unwanted emotions you've been collecting over the years.

At the beginning of this section I shared the hopeless state of my inbox and the unlikelihood of ever getting it under control. Although I've compared this inbox with your inner being inbox, there is one significant difference. Your inner inbox is much easier to clean, and it's much more rewarding to do so. In my experience, cleaning out the negative emotions from your inner inbox is the most life-changing and significant self-work you can do. Just because this process creates some of the biggest most positive life changes you'll ever see, don't be fooled into believing this process needs to take months or years to accomplish. In future chapters, you'll learn various techniques that will help you release the emotions you've collected. If you're unsure about which negative emotions you've been collecting that's ok too, as we'll also explore powerful identification techniques.

Emotions Power Behavior

When out and about at social events I like to play a fun little game where I surprise friends with how much I can tell about them and their upbringing by getting tiny tidbits of information about their current circumstances. For example, during an engaging discussion around the nature of behaviour, my friend Peter asked me why he was so career focused and such a hard worker, to the point where it was almost a flaw.

My response went something like this. I told Peter that his obsession with hard work and career likely came from the amount of pressure he put on himself when it came to the importance of achievement. That pressure might manifest as tense muscles or physical problems in his upper back, neck, or shoulders. I told him he might also suffer from powerlessness and lower back issues that often go along with feelings of never being good enough. His driving nature for success might be rooted in the belief that he needed to prove himself or needed to be perfect in order to remain safe. This is a common pattern in individuals who grew up being bullied in school or bullied in a physical or emotional way by a parent. Often they feel the need to be perfect to protect themselves and not become a target. I went on to say that Peter might have grown up with a parent who not only wasn't nurturing, but who was also emotionally controlling or highly judgemental or critical and that he had likely felt nothing was ever good enough for that parent. This might have made Peter feel rejected and unloved and made him seek achievement as a way of earning their love.

Peter looked at me with eyes wide open. He couldn't believe the accuracy of my analysis and let me know what I had said was spot on.

All of our behaviour, from perfectionism to the way we treat ourselves and other people, is rooted in our emotional baggage and beliefs. Although we're always collecting emotions and beliefs based on our experiences, it's under the age of seven when we're the most programmable. The way your parents made you feel, the circumstances you observed at a young age, and the emotional baggage you picked up during that time, and still carry, is likely the biggest unconscious driving force of your life. Have you ever wondered why you've picked up the same circumstances or patterns of behaviour you witnessed in your parents? If so, it's possible you've picked up the same emotional baggage your parents were carrying while you were under their care.

As an adult do you feel as though you have a hard time fitting in?

Do you feel like you're not loveable?

Do you have an incessant need to be perfect?

Do you feel like everyone is watching and judging you?

Do you feel the need to prove yourself?

Do you treat others in ways you regret or wish were different?

Do you feel as though nobody supports you?

Do you have negative perspectives around money or relationships?

If you answered yes to any of these questions, spend a few seconds reflecting on your childhood or past circumstances to see how you may have picked up these feelings.

How do these feelings impact our behaviour? They create discomfort deep inside of us that we look to sooth through outer world action, by trying to control and manipulate our circumstances. A good example of this is people who are always fighting for a cause. In my province of residence, there has been a big anti-fracking movement with a number of recent protests as a gas company tried to establish fracking operations in the area. Although most of the public is in general agreement that fracking should be banned, not everyone attends the rallies and protest. Most of those present are there because they want to prevent fracking from taking place in their own back yard, but a small handful of individuals are there not just because they want fracking banned, but because they like to protest. These individuals jump from rally to rally, protest to protest because they like fighting for a cause.

Although these causes are likely worthy of protest, I would contend that the protesters are being driven to action by a feeling that resides deep inside their state of being. The feeling that drives them is likely that of being suppressed and controlled and if I could have an open discussion with these protesters, they would most likely share that they grew up in a highly suppressive environment where they felt dominated and controlled by an influential figure.

Protesting may bring temporary relief for the emotions they are carrying around as baggage, but until the underlying negative emotions are dealt with, they will continue to seek a better feeling place through their actions. Until they properly deal with the emotions in their inbox that are driving their behaviour, these feelings will remain.

THE POWER OF JOY

OUR EMOTIONAL STATE DRIVES our behaviour, but have you ever taken the time to reflect on the actual purpose of emotions? Could they exist for any reason other than simply needing to be felt?

When I first started to write this book my laptop was old and falling apart. Even though it had lasted for over five years - longer than any other machine I had owned - it was time to let it go. It took nearly two weeks for my new purchase to arrive and I was excited to plug it in and get to work. After a few hours of testing out my new computer I noticed something strange. My internet connection was dreadfully slow.

After a little investigation I realized that the wireless network card in my new machine had incredibly poor connectivity. If I was more than 15 feet away from the router, the signal strength of my connection would be at a zero. Although I can still write without an internet connection I can't do all the other things that support me in my writing. When sitting at my desk I was disconnected. This meant I no longer had access to my online thesaurus, or my online journal where I keep my notes, or my streaming music service that allows me to play the binaural beats that keep me focused.

All the tools critical to supporting me in my writing endeavour, the things that make my life as a writer much easier, were inaccessible. Gone.

Luckily I was able to connect with the manufacturer's support team and find a resolution to my poor Wi-Fi signal. I also appreciated the experience as it gave me one of my favourite analogies.

Just like a computer has an internet signal between it and the wireless router, providing your computer with a plethora of tools to make your life easier, you have a connection to something even more powerful than the internet: your inner being. The level of joy you are experiencing in any given moment, represents the level of connectivity that exists between you and your inner being. The happier and more joyful you are, in any given moment, the more in tune and connected you are with your soul.

Why is this important? Because a strong and stable connection with your inner being changes everything.

A number of years ago I remember noticing how, depending on the day, circumstances would play out very differently. On some days I would go into the office and everything would flow with more ease than I could imagine. The right people would send me what I needed at just the right times. The answers to all my questions would magically pop into my mind with little to no effort. It was as if everything I needed was finding me instead of me needing to go out and find it. Green lights, and the best parking spots, and my favourite songs playing on the radio, all flowed to me with ease.

Other days, I'd experience the exact opposite. Nothing would get done on time. Getting work completed would be a struggle and I'd feel very unproductive. Things would go wrong, systems would crash and I'd just want to go home and go back to bed.

At the time I was studying the law of attraction and different theories about our reality, so it made sense to start keeping track of details. Why was it that some days flowed with ease while others were a complete struggle? Was it simply random, or was there a trigger responsible for creating good or bad days? One day, it hit me.

The days that flowed with ease, the good days, were of course the days where I felt amazing, when I was incredibly happy and joyful. The bad days, not so much. One of the books I was reading was *The Law of Attraction* by Abraham-Hicks who, in a nutshell, teach us that our outer world experience is a reflection of our inner state of being; that our thoughts and feelings create our reality.

Was I feeling happy on the good days because things were going so well? Or, as taught by the law of attraction, were the days flowing with ease because I already felt good?

These were still early days in personal development for me. I had not yet mastered my ability to be happy and joyful, as I have learned to do over the last few years. However, what I now know without a doubt is that those happy days, which flowed with ease, were a direct response to the way I felt on a given day.

That was one of my first concrete examples of what has become a cornerstone of my belief system. The happier I feel, and the more I find myself in a state of joy, the more my life unfolds in magical ways.

In the introduction to this book I eluded to a secret ingredient. The key to what allowed me to completely transform my life and begin to live the life I know I was meant to be living. That secret ingredient is **joy**.

Abraham-Hicks teaches us that a greater part of us resides in the non-physical. I'm not exactly sure what this greater part is, whether it's our soul, inner being, source energy, all that is, or God. It doesn't matter what we call it or how we view it, but what does matter, is that we know it exists.

Accepting the existence of this greater force is difficult for most people. It hasn't been proven by science and it may never be. You can hear other people's experiences with this force but the only way you can truly believe is to experience it for yourself.

Take a minute and reflect on how your days play out. Do you often experience states of flow or has struggle and effort become the norm? The amount of flow you experience directly relates to the amount of joy you are capable of achieving and all of that flows from the connection between you and your inner being.

Think of the times where you've experienced flow and see if you can notice a pattern. Take notice how great you felt early in the morning on those days, before you even noticed you were in flow. And on the days that didn't turn out so great? You likely had negative emotional momentum going on before you even had breakfast.

Whether you want to admit it, realize it or not, a bigger part of you in the non-physical has your back and is always present behind the scenes. It's there guiding you down your path. It's bringing to you the things you desire. However, unless you're consistently in a state of joy, your connection isn't strong enough to receive the guidance and support being provided by it.

Just as I struggled to write without my Wi-Fi connection to the internet, most people are struggling with their lives because of their lack of connection to their inner being.

Life 2.0

What happens when you're able to live your life fully connected to your inner being? Life becomes filled with incredible synchronicities lining up almost unbelievable events, all of which play out in your favour. Achieving this high signal strength, by being in joy, is what is responsible for putting you in a state known as "flow."

When you begin to consistently achieve states of flow you will come to realize how powerful universal forces are and how magical life can be. It's true confirmation that you are not alone and that we are all connected and fully supported by a higher power. You get a pure sense, a knowing, that this is how life is meant to be lived and experienced. It's what I call the next evolution of the human experience, or Life 2.0.

When you are living in flow you're making a shift from a life where struggle is the norm to one where ease becomes the biggest part of your daily experience. Flow puts you in a complete co-creative state with the universe. As you continue to experience flow you completely transform the way you view and experience your reality. The more you maintain your state of joy the more frequent the synchronicities you experience. Over time you develop such a great sense of trust in your experiences that you will learn to let go of the need to control your outer world and its circumstances.

Keep in mind that being in flow doesn't mean you won't experience contrasting or challenging life experiences. What it does mean is that when those more difficult life circumstances arise, you're also greeted with a high level of support and understanding that allows you to flow through these experiences with much greater ease.

In the summer of 2014, after taking six weeks of vacation, I had the inspiration to write an eBook that became the foundation for my two-day in person master class and online program. I had toyed with the idea of writing a book for a while but up until this point the writing process had been a struggle. The inspiration just wasn't there and any effort seemed futile. I was expecting a number of guests over the summer so I decided to take the summer months off and dedicated my time to family and friends. I spent each morning lying on the beach, doing whatever felt best that day, relaxing and having fun without a care in the world. After the first few weeks I felt amazing, and that's when something shifted. Inspiration kicked in and I started to write.

Within six weeks the entire book was written. The best part? The universe had thrown in a synchronicity to help me out. As it turned out a lovely lady who just happened to be an author with editing experience was renting a cottage just three houses down the street. Not only was she experienced in writing and editing but also was a huge fan of the law of attraction, attended Abraham-Hicks seminars, and was well versed in my subject matter. She ended up giving me a very reasonable price and did an amazing job helping me out with the book.

The story perfectly exemplifies how seeking joy opened up a creative flow state that brought the inspiration for my writing. It also demonstrates that synchronicities are not only possible, but can be expected, when operating in states of flow, as I've gotten better and better at achieving states of flow, this type of synchronicity has become a common occurrence in my life. Part of evolving to this next level of human experience is learning to hand over control to your inner being. Let it connect the dots and make things happen, allowing you to kick back and put your focus on being happy and seeking joy.

The more I live in, and experience. states of flow, the more I realize that it's not our role or responsibility to solve our problems. When we connect with our inner beings through the feeling of joy, solutions to problems tend to present themselves with little effort. This doesn't mean that tough decisions don't need to be made or action never needs to be taken. What it does mean is that if you can feel good before anything else, the easiest and most obvious course of action becomes much more apparent.

You Are Always Being Guided

At different times in my life, I've felt stuck. Not just stuck in terms of feeling I had nowhere to go, but stuck in terms of not being exactly sure where to point my sails. Feeling as though I wasn't going anywhere and didn't know how to move out of my situation was one of the most discouraging places to be. Unfortunately, most people can relate. It's very common for me to hear from individuals who tell me they feel lost in life. They are seeking out their purpose but are having no success. They sense they have a calling yet feel as though they can't figure out what it is or how to find it.

The solution? Follow the guidance of your inner being.

Your inner being is always guiding you. It knows exactly where you want to go even before you consciously become aware of it. It knows the best possible path to your desire. The problem, however, is that you may not be able to see the path laid out in front of you. You're unaware of, or may not be tuned into, the signals being sent. Because you're out of alignment and disconnected, you're not receiving the messages or just not tuning in.

How does your inner being guide you? Intuition is one of the principle forms of guidance, however, there is another one that is much more readily accessible: your emotional state. Your inner being, like a GPS, knows the quickest and most effective route to any desired state. It's always communicating with you. Guiding you. Not through a digital screen, but through the way you feel, using your emotions. Emotions are the highest form of intuition.

In the same way that your inner being is giving you intuitive nudges, it's also feeding you positive and negative feeling emotions. When you fully tune in to your intuition it will never fail you. The same is the case for your emotions.

Does a thought about a specific course of action excite you? Does it feel good? If so, your inner being is in agreement with your thoughts. It wants you to proceed down this path. That's where it wants you to put your focus. Each little bit of excitement you feel is a breadcrumb leading you down the path to your greatest desires.

Conversely, does a specific thought bring up anxiety or does a certain decision feel bad? When an unpleasant feeling surfaces, this is your inner being telling you it's not in harmony with what you're thinking. By ignoring this feeling you're essentially disregarding your inner being's guidance. Your inner GPS is telling you that you should turn left, yet you decide to go right instead.

Are you able to recall a time in your life when you had a hunch or a feeling that something was a bad decision? Even with this hunch you decided to ignore it and go through with the decision anyways? How did that circumstance work out for you?

Your inner being is always present. It is always guiding you. Consciously honour the way you feel with regard to the choices you make. The more you listen and tune in to your emotions the more you benefit from the guidance being presented to you. By simply tuning in to your emotions, both positive and negative, you'll gain a powerful ally in the way you experience your life.

Your inner being is the highest form of guidance you will ever receive. It is specifically programmed for you and nobody else. If you can accurately tune into the guidance of your inner being and properly interpret the messages it is sending to you, that guidance can be your primary source of direction. Without a doubt, I would follow the guidance it provides above all else. Your strong intuitive channels and the guidance you receive through feelings will never fail you. How does this all relate to your path and purpose?

Those unable to connect to their path or who feel lost in life find themselves in this state because they aren't hearing the guidance of their inner being. It isn't that this guidance isn't present. But the connection between them and their inner being is too weak for them to receive it. Sometimes, this is due to fears and beliefs that stand in the way and prevent hearing and acting on the guidance being received. The path is always present, but it's up to you to find an emotional state that allows you to become aware of it.

Not everyone is aware of the presence of a higher power or their inner being. Until proven by science, most people may never believe. If you have a hard time believing, just remember that there are many aspects of our reality that can't be seen, tasted, touched, heard, or smelled by humans. Radio waves, cell phone connections, and even the oxygen we breathe are all examples. We know these things are present and always around us, even though we can't see them. The same is true for our inner being.

Gaining the awareness of my inner being didn't happen over night. It took time and years of experience to build the confidence and knowing that it's always present, that it always has my back, and that it's always guiding me, no matter how well I'm listening. Harnessing the relationship with my inner being is the single most powerful, life-changing thing I've done. In fact, I can't imagine anything that could have a more significant impact on my experience. Although the words in this book may help you gain awareness, experience is the only true teacher. The perspective you take on the presence of your inner being or a higher power is your choice. You can choose to believe that something you can't see doesn't exist. Or, you can give it the benefit of the doubt, consider the possibility, and work on developing your awareness of it in the hopes of bettering your life.

When we live our lives fully connected with our inner being not only does our path and purpose become apparent, but life also becomes easy. Life flows. We experience life in a whole new way. We live life the way it is truly meant to be lived.

YOUR GUIDE TO INNER GUIDANCE

SHORTLY AFTER THE BIRTH of my daughter I was presented with an opportunity that involved an important life decision. The family beach house property, owned by my grandparents, who were in their nineties, was going up for sale. This cottage was on a prime piece of land along the ocean right on the beach. Growing up, I spent time there most summers and the idea of giving the same opportunity to my children excited me. Purchasing the cottage came with the condition that my father and his siblings had no interest in the property. It also came with the significant financial implications of owning a second home.

After meeting with family members my father informed me that the cottage could be mine. I was only given a short amount of time to make my decision, and was torn. I decided to meditate in the hopes of gaining the insight needed to make my decision.

After thirty minutes of what I hoped would be clarity inducing meditation, I opened my eyes. I hadn't received the immediate answer I was looking for. As I stood up to make my way to the kitchen I heard a bing from my laptop, indicating I had received a new message in my inbox. Walking over to the screen I noticed that it was a new Twitter follower notification. The individual who followed my account was not someone I personally knew. The profile description read: "Family man who loves nature and spending time living on the beach relaxing with his family and friends."

Based on past experiences, and the number of synchronicities I experience in my life, I knew this was the answer I was looking for. I asked and my inner being gave me a clear answer. As previously mentioned it took me years to learn how to fully tune into my inner guidance. This doesn't necessarily mean that tuning in is difficult or takes years of work. It's something anyone, including you, can start doing as soon as today! Now that you're aware of the fact that you have this universal guidance always guiding and supporting you, you're already halfway there.

Passion and Excitement

The strongest guidance you'll ever receive is in the form of feelings. No feeling should ever be ignored and the feeling you should pay the most attention to is passion. The things you are passionate about and enjoy doing to the point where you lose track of time are those things your inner being wants you to give the most attention to. Passion and excitement are the highest form of communication and should never be ignored. The things you are passionate about are the things that are in full alignment with you at the deepest levels.

Have you ever noticed that the individuals who are the most successful in life are those who are passionate about what they do? It's not a coincidence that when you follow your passion it becomes easier to maintain a state of joy and achieve great levels of success. This is when you're co-creating with your inner being at the highest level.

Excitement is also guidance from your inner being. In any given moment your inner being is guiding you down your optimal path through excitement. It could be excitement about a job opportunity, a course you'd like to sign up for, or moving to a new home. The excitement could even be for smaller circumstances such as talking to a friend, stopping in at a coffee shop, or visiting a thrift store. I can't tell you how many times Anik has had sudden urges to randomly visit thrift shops only to miraculously find an exact designer piece of clothing she's been looking for.

One of the most conscious, life-changing choices you can make is to allow your life to be guided by excitement. At any moment in time, ask yourself what the most exciting thing is that you can do, and follow the trail of excitement.

Intuition

Intuition, when properly interpreted, is never wrong. That time you picked up the phone knowing who was on the other end even before answering, or that time you swerved your vehicle or slammed on the brake pedal seconds before any signs of danger are both examples of intuitive nudges from your inner being.

Everyone has equal ability to tune into their intuition and follow their inner guidance, however, few people are actually doing it. It's not a thing that is readily discussed in mainstream society and it often goes ignored. I consider intuition to be a sense, like seeing, hearing, or tasting. The more you use it, the stronger your intuition gets. Your level of joy is also a factor; the happier you are, the more capable you are of receiving those messages from your inner being.

When it comes to the development of intuition, people receive messages in various ways. Some people hear voices in their mind, which they can somehow differentiate from their own inner thoughts. Usually just a word or random passing thought, this form of intuition is known as clairaudience. My clairaudience is weaker than my other forms of intuition, however, I do, on occasion, pick up random bits of thought that I recognize as being slightly different from my regular thought patterns. When I notice these words or thoughts I make sure to give them extra attention.

My strongest form of intuition, and what I believe to be the most common, is claircognizance. This is simply a gut feeling or a knowing, that often appears out of the blue. This form of intuition is the one that usually helps us slam on the brakes and prevent a near accident, or the one that guides us down a specific street or path helping us find something we've been looking for. I find the best way to differentiate intuitive knowing from thoughts created by the mind is by acknowledging that intuitive knowing feels like it often comes from your gut or your chest and is likely the source of the common term "a gut feeling."

A third common form of intuition is clairvoyance. Clairvoyance is a form of intuition used by your inner being to communicate to you through an image in your mind. Clairvoyant flashes are often difficult to pick up because they only last a split second. A good way to differentiate a clairvoyant message from other thoughts or imagination is through the random nature of the image. Often times these images may be symbolic in nature and difficult to decode. For example, your inner being may use images of animals that have different totem meanings (you can look these meanings up online).

One morning I remember asking my inner being for guidance on a specific subject. Later that day during a silent meditation I had a brief flash of the image of a grasshopper. Upon looking up the totem meaning of grasshopper I had read that it was symbolic for moving forward. This was the answer for which I had been looking.

When it comes to intuition the most important suggestion I can make is for you to pay attention. Like a chef learning to recognize the smell of each spice in a bowl of soup, it takes time and practice. The more you listen, the more you pick up the intuitive cues and nudges provided by your inner being and the easier it will get.

Synchronicities

Synchronicities are another important form of guidance from your inner being. These are events that occur in our lives that we often call coincidences. Those who are spiritually aware know that nothing in life is a coincidence. A common form of synchronicity is recurring number patterns such as 11:11 or 12:34. Often, these number patterns occur at various important times in our life. I see these as our inner being trying to get our attention or to call our awareness to what it is we're thinking about.

Pay attention to songs with meaningful lyrics, as they can be another form of synchronicity through which your inner being may communicate. On occasion, when looking for the answer to a specific question, my mind would suddenly bring my attention to a song playing on the radio, or I'd wake up with certain song lyrics repeating in my head. Often times, the lyrics would have surprising relevance to an answer I'd been seeking to a specific question or situation in my life. Not all songs are messages, and I usually combine these answers with other forms of awareness before coming to a conclusion. Nonetheless, these are fun ways to gain clarity while tuning in to your inner being.

There are numerous forms of synchronicities occurring every day, if you're paying attention. Has a friend ever offered to lend you the exact book you've been meaning to purchase but just haven't found the time? Or maybe you meet a massage therapist by chance, just hours after asking your inner being for the best course of action to resolve a shoulder pain issue. Not all synchronicities are mind-blowing and dramatic; some are subtle. When you begin to keep your eye out for these types of events and follow their lead, you'll soon start to realize how these events are more than just coincidence.

Drop Expectations

Often times we follow our inner guidance with certain expectations that don't always play out. In this case you may have a tendency to think your inner guidance has failed you.

It hasn't. Your inner guidance, when properly interpreted, is never wrong.

Your inner being has a much broader perspective of your reality than your conscious mind. Although a certain coincidental encounter may have not played out the way you were hoping, this encounter may have been coordinated for a completely different reason that you're not yet aware of. Maybe you've synchronistically met someone who you thought was your soul mate only to be stood up. Although this could feel like your inner being has failed you, it might be that this event helped bring to the surface emotions that needed to be dealt with. This way, you'll be in a better mental and emotional place to attract that partner you really want.

Is it okay to have dreams and expectations? Absolutely. However, it's not your job to figure out how to bring these dreams and expectations to realization. That's the role of your inner being. Often times I'll work with individuals who only see one specific path to a goal, and when that path doesn't play out, their limiting beliefs keep them stuck and prevent them from seeing the path their inner being *is* guiding them down.

When following inner guidance understand that your inner being is always guiding you down the best possible path to your desires. This path won't always make sense to your rational mind until you reach the destination. The more you allow yourself to trust the path, the easier it becomes for your inner being to guide you down it.

Get Happy

As mentioned in previous sections, joy is key. The more consistently you can remain in a state of joy, the stronger your connection with your inner being becomes and the more you will experience its inner guidance.

Know Your Blockers

The first step in following the inner guidance being provided to you is learning how to tune in and receive the messages. The second is not allowing your mind to block that guidance by creating fear and doubt.

Often individuals are hearing the guidance provided by their inner being, yet they don't act upon the guidance they receive due to fears and limiting beliefs. It's not uncommon to be working with individuals who might feel excited by something, but whose ego creates a barrier that keeps them from their path. For example, people who've experienced a traumatic disappointment at some point in life, may not even allow themselves to get excited for fear of getting disappointed again. I've worked with women on multiple occasions who have remained single for over a decade, not because of their bad dating skills or level of attractiveness, but because of a past traumatic relationship. Being cheated on by someone you love, for example, may scare your ego to the point where it feels unsafe to date or enter a relationship, regardless of how much excitement or attraction may be present.

Doubt can also prevent you from following your guidance. Many people discount certain encounters as coincidence or don't follow through on intuitive nudges because they can't see the potential benefit from a rational standpoint. Try giving the guidance you receive the benefit of the doubt. You never know what surprises are waiting around the corner!

ASK AND IT IS GIVEN

Not only is your inner being always communicating to you, it's also always listening.

I recently woke up to what started as an ordinary morning. I did my morning appreciation journaling and went downstairs to grab a tea before doing the rest of my morning routine. As the kettle began to boil, I hit the off switch and reached for my favorite chamomile tea. From the corner of my eye I noticed through the window, about twenty feet in front of me on top of a rock, what looked like the biggest seagull I had ever seen. I turned my head to get a closer look and saw not a seagull, but a big white snowy owl staring right at me as if it were peering into my soul.

The owl is one of my totem animals and not only had I never seen an owl in the wild before, but I had never seen a bird this utterly magnificent. I was in complete awe.

I ran to the office to grab my camera as I was yelling to Anik upstairs to quickly look out the window. I made it back to the window in time and snapped a shot of the owl a few moments before it took off down the beach.

Later that morning, once I regained my composure, I took a walk down the beach to see if he was still hanging around. Off into the distance I saw a white spec along the wharf. As I got closer my suspicions were confirmed, it was indeed my friend. As I approached, I noticed there wasn't one, but rather two owls perched along the wharf wall! They allowed me to snap a few pictures from about 15 feet away before they gracefully flew off into the distance.

I'll always remember my owl encounter, not only because of the magic that exuded from these beautiful birds, but also because they were a manifestation of an intention I had set a few days prior.

During my morning journaling I'll often do some intention setting though the form of a question, something I'll be teaching you in the next section. A few days prior to the owl encounter I was focused on wanting to build my online community so that I would have a bigger audience when promoting my book. The first logical thing that came to mind was to have something I post on Facebook go viral and reach as many people as possible. I had written: "What would it take for a Facebook post to go viral and reach more people than I've ever reached before?"

How does this relate to the owl who came by for a visit?

The pictures of the owl I had taken that morning, which I posted on my Facebook wall, got more likes and shares than anything else I had ever posted on my personal Facebook page.

My inner being, as it always does, heard my call and delivered a viral post. The only problem is that my request wasn't specific enough. What I should have asked for was how to have a post related to my business go viral. This was a great lesson in how our inner beings take what we say literally and also a reminder to be as specific as possible when making requests.

Your inner being is always listening to you. Taking time out of my day to communicate with mine is an important part of my morning routine and, I know, would be a welcome addition to yours. Whether through prayer, vision boards, journaling, or talking to yourself out loud, the most important part is putting lots of emotion into your message. Your entire reality is feeding off of the way you feel.

Abraham-Hicks teaches that it only takes seventeen seconds of focus to begin building the momentum for a desire and that after only sixty-eight seconds of intense focus, your desire is on its way to you. No need to spend hours focusing on a desire and no need to create the most beautiful vision board on your block. The simple instructions I give most of my clients is to write the story of the desire as if it's already been made manifest, spend 15 minutes in meditation painting and feeling this picture, then let it go. The rest of the work? Get out of your own way by dealing with the emotions and beliefs preventing you from allowing the desire to show up.

WHY THIS NOW

A FEW YEARS AGO I started working one-on-one with clients and something strange began to occur. A large number of my clients - well over half - were cancelling bookings within 24 hours of their scheduled sessions. They would book, but wouldn't commit to showing up. This went on for a number of months and eventually, using techniques you'll learn later in this book, I figured out why. The reasons for the cancellations not only blew my mind, but also confirmed something I had theorized for a while.

The circumstances in your outer reality are a direct reflection of your inner state of being.

Most people who've watched The Secret or read books on the law of attraction believe that in order to manifest a desire you need to put all your focus on it. You need to set your intent, do affirmations, and put together a vision board. These are all great exercises, however, when it comes to the law of attraction, most people are missing the most important point.

Every single circumstance in your life, both wanted and unwanted, is a manifestation. Abraham-Hicks defines the law of attraction to be a law, just like gravity, where the vibration you're putting out, through your thoughts and feelings, is being reflected back to you in your life circumstances.

What does that mean? Every circumstance, from your love life, to your financial situation, career, and even your health, is a reflection of what's going on inside of you. Through the law of attraction you can change any circumstance in your life by shifting the thoughts you think and the way you feel.

During the time that I was working with these clients I had been separated from my ex-wife for about a year and a half. I had never doubted my decision to leave; it felt right and I had no regrets. I felt happy in my personal life, as well as with my decision. The emotional turmoil that went with leaving what was supposed to be a life-long commitment seemed to be behind me. As I was reflecting on the situation with my client cancellations, I started to dig into my inner being and the baggage I was carrying. Like an unnoticed cobweb I found something hidden in one of the corners. An emotion I was unaware I had clung to: the fear that I might be unable to commit.

I pulled some of the emotional clearing tools out of my tool belt. I worked on clearing the emotion along with a few others that came up in the process. What happened next?

Like magic, almost overnight, the issue with my clients not committing to their appointments completely went away. I previously hinted that this book would change how you perceive your reality. How? By learning that the emotions you've been carrying in your inner inbox don't only impact the way you feel, they also alter your entire life experience. Your emotional state impacts every single circumstance that occurs in your life.

One of my favourite concepts shared by Dalai Lama is that we can never maintain peace in the outer world, until we make peace within ourselves. I love this concept, not only because it promotes inner peace, but also because what he is saying is true in a literal sense.

When your inner inbox is cluttered with strong feelings of powerlessness, you'll attract unwanted situations that make you feel powerless. If you're holding a great deal of anger from the past, you'll attract circumstances that will continue to anger you. The more negative emotions you carry, the more difficult your life becomes because your reality is reflecting these emotions back to you through the circumstances it creates.

A secondary way your reality is reflected back to you is through your focus. Wherever you're putting your attention is an invitation to bring more of that into your reality. I've always been aware of the concept that "you get what you think about" but only recently did I realize the importance of controlling where you put your focus thanks to a bunch of bees.

This past July I was busily trimming the grass around our vegetable garden raised beds. Thanks to all the beautiful vegetable plants beginning to flower, there seemed to be a large number of bees flying around and I was doing my best to avoid getting stung. Unaware that a nest was present, I inadvertently swung the trimmer over a hole in the ground and a handful of bees came rushing out of a hole and straight at me! I quickly dropped my trimmer, dashed across the yard, and was lucky to get stung only twice.

Although the pain was brief, this created an interesting phenomenon for the rest of the summer. I saw bees everywhere. Not wanting to get stung again, I was always on the lookout for them, which, thanks to the law of attraction, multiplied their appearance in my reality. I would be lying on the deck in the sun and bees would land on my swim trunks and walk around before taking off again. Or, I would be swimming almost one hundred meters out into the ocean and a bee would fly right by me!

Although this story doesn't necessarily relate to you unless you have a strong fear of bees, a more common example of where unwanted focus may be impacting your reality, is with money.

Two of the most common areas where people look to apply the law of attraction in their lives are relationships and finances. When it comes to money, most people seem to be stuck because they're carrying around emotions around a lack of money, which extends out into lack of freedom, lack of control, and powerlessness.

When you focus on the lack of anything, thanks to the law of attraction, you'll attract more lack. What does this mean? You need to work on where you put your focus. This can be hard as a human since we've got a natural tendency to place our focus on our problems, when in reality, we should be focusing on those things that feel good. I'll be teaching you how to do this later in this book.

Knowing you get what you focus on isn't all bad. Once you learn to be more conscious of your focus point and begin to control it, you can use it to your advantage. For example, I spent a month playing the lottery where I was putting an extra amount of focus on winning tickets. Although during those four weeks I never had a winning ticket over twenty dollars, I did win on ten of twelve tickets, thereby beating the odds by a long shot.

What You Resist Will Persist

When was the last time you needed to remember the name of a person, or a place, but couldn't? You focus so intently and try as hard as you possibly can to remember that name. Yet, it continues to remain just out of reach. A little later you no longer need it, and you've completely switched your attention to something else. You're not even thinking about remembering the name when suddenly, out of the blue, it randomly pops into your head.

With zero focus or effort. Complete ease. Without even trying!

How many couples do you know who've had difficulty conceiving? I've known a number who, after adopting or giving up on conceiving, became pregnant. These types of stories happen more often than seems rationally possible. The explanation? Those involved let go of the emotional state - in this case, often desperation - that is causing resistance that then blocks the manifestation, or the reality they so acutely want.

Can you remember a time in your life when you decided to let go of a desire? Maybe you stopped caring or gave up out of frustration. What happened when you stopped giving it any attention? The most likely answer? Your desire showed up!

The one thing preventing you from manifesting anything you want in life is resistance. The source of the resistance is your thoughts and feelings.

The example of not remembering a name may seem simplistic, however it perfectly exemplifies how your entire reality is shaped. Not just your ability to remember names and places, but also the reality of how you manifest all the things that enter your life. Every desire in your outer world, is handed to you by the universe, when your state of being has achieved the correct frequency; a frequency of no resistance which allows your inner state of being to perfectly align with that desire.

What does this have to do with joy and your emotions? Everything.

Those who experience the successful manifestation of their desires do so because they've changed their thoughts and feelings, the changing of which then released the resistance that was preventing the outer world manifestation. By letting go of negative emotions, they've shifted their focus away from the perceived problem, allowing the universe to step in, take over, and make things happen.

Teal Scott said it best with the following quote:

"I must feel good to manifest what I want, but now that I feel good I don't care about getting it and voilà ... there it is!"

The only thing that prevents you from allowing your desires to manifest is you - more specifically, it's the thoughts and feelings you hold in relation to *not* having your desire, the belief that it won't show up, and any desperation or pressure you feel to have things be *different* so you can feel better. The more desperation that exists in your state of being, the more you kink your receiving hose. The more your hose is kinked, the more you prevent the desire from entering your physical experience.

The solution? Stop putting so much focus on controlling outer world needs in order to achieve the feelings you want to feel. Let go of needing to acquire a specific job, relationship, house, or money to feel good. Instead, work directly on taking control of your emotional state. Seek joy. By successfully achieving your chosen feeling state, without being dependant on the realization of your desires to make that state a reality, you release resistance. Removing the pressure of needing to experience the outside circumstance and unconditionally shifting your state of being unclogs your receiving hose. The end result? Your receiving hose opens and the manifestation appears.

Simple, right? You need only to learn how to consistently achieve your desired feeling state in the absence of those things that you want (better relationships, more money, getting pregnant, etc.) and you open the floodgates to receiving! If you're not sure how to do this, don't worry! The entire process, along with action steps, is outlined in the following pages.

Why This Now?

For many, it can come as an unsettling realization to discover that our outer reality is a reflection of our inner state of being - especially if we've always believed the complete opposite to be true! But as we relax into it, the knowledge that we can learn to control our entire reality by learning to control our mental and emotional states, can instill in us a sense of extreme empowerment.

Anytime an unwanted or unexpected circumstance presents itself, ask yourself the question "why this now?" Asking yourself what part of you created this experience will help you transcend it. Was it something you created by giving it too much attention through focus? Is it something that brings up a pattern of emotion? By taking ownership of your circumstances, you can then turn inwards so you can learn how to shift them. I'll be giving you specific processes to help you with these steps later in the book.

EVOLUTION OF THE HUMAN EXPERIENCE

LAST YEAR I VISITED a friend who had just moved into a new apartment. He explained that he'd been dealing with ants since moving in (about three months prior), yet hadn't determined how they were getting in. I suggested we solve the problem by shifting the way he felt in order to alter his attraction point with a desired end result of shifting this outer world circumstance.

I quickly explained how he was attracting this situation through his emotional state and that shifting his state of being would help with his ant problem. He agreed to try. I asked him how the ant situation made him feel and he responded, "frustrated." Like a magnet, the frustration in his inbox was attracting frustrating experiences, like the ants. I informed him we had to clear the emotion of frustration from his attraction point. Once cleared, his ant situation would resolve itself — either the ants would simply disappear, or a solution would find him.

We spent twenty minutes doing emotional clearing using EFT (a tool we'll dive into later in this book) to clear frustration and various related aspects. I told him to expect a resolution to his problem within the next few weeks. Five days later he contacted me. His six-year-old son, while playing with a toy car along a wall, found the exact place where the ants were coming in. Not only that, but there was also putty (to cover the hole) left next to the opening by the previous tenant.

By shifting the contents of his attraction point the solution to the problem found him. He was unable to control his outer world circumstance, yet by shifting his inner world, the outer world soon followed.

The concept of the "attraction point" is one of my favourite concepts coming from the law of attraction. When you purchase a new vehicle, you get the luxury of receiving an owner's manual explaining all of the lights, buzzers and buttons, and how to get the most out of your vehicle. When you enter the physical plane and pop through the birth canal, you're unfortunately left to figure out this reality on your own. If there were a book entitled "How to Get the Most Out of Your Reality," the first and most important chapter would be about the attraction point.

The most vital realization you can make is that your entire reality, every single circumstance that you experience, is one you've attracted. Everything that occurs, both wanted and unwanted, is a reflection of your state of being; more specifically, of the contents of your attraction point.

Scary? Perhaps. Empowering? Absolutely!

Take a moment to fully absorb and let this in. Let me repeat it for you: You have full control over your reality and everything that takes place within it.

The catch? Control isn't exercised through external means, by manipulating the circumstances and events around you through action. Control is exercised by managing your attraction point, by consciously fine-tuning what you think and how you feel, and by managing what's going on deep inside of you.

You control the circumstances in your outer world, by shifting aspects of your inner world.

The best way to understand your attraction point is through the concept of a radio receiver. By turning the knob on your radio you can change frequencies and select different channels. If you want a different station, you need to switch to another frequency by turning the knob. You're also tuning into a specific frequency via your attraction point. This frequency is based on the thoughts and feelings you are choosing to experience. Like radio waves from a radio tower, your thoughts and feelings are being broadcast from your inner being out into the universe. And just like the receiver in your home or car turns those radio waves into beautiful music, your thoughts and feelings are being received by the material of the universe and molded into realities and life circumstances that match the emotions and beliefs in your attraction point.

When it came to my clients not committing to their sessions I resolved the problem by letting go of my own feelings of being non-committal. By releasing my emotions around lack of commitment, I shifted my attraction point to a new frequency. This shifted my reality to a new set of circumstances where the problem was no longer occurring.

What does this mean exactly?

If your inner being's inbox is filled with feelings of frustration and anger, the universe will respond to you by creating circumstances that will frustrate and anger you. If you believe you will never find true love, odds are you never will. If you have low self-worth you'll likely attract relationships that make you feel unworthy. The more you believe a situation will occur, the higher the odds of it occurring. The stronger you feel an emotion at a conscious or subconscious level, the more you will attract situations reflecting that emotion.

Your entire physical reality has always been, and always will be, a construct of your inner state of being. Your thoughts, feelings, conscious, and subconscious, all combined. They are the driving forces of the wanted and unwanted aspects in your life. Your physical reality is reflecting back to you, like a mirror, your state of being.

You can shift any situation in your life by shifting your state of being to a new frequency.

Becoming aware of the fact that you have an attraction point changes your approach to the circumstances in your life. By gaining this awareness you come to understand not only the importance your thoughts and feelings but also the ease with which you can easily shift your life circumstances by shifting your state of being!

Allow life to flow with ease, follow the path that best serves you, and stop trying to figure everything out! By rationally trying to discern the proximity and location of your desires, you're essentially trying to cut your own path through the jungle, not realizing that a path has already been laid out for you. A path that has been specifically tailored to your desires. A path that will effortlessly take you where you want to go with absolute ease. The path has always been there, it will always be there; you simply need to tune into your inner being so you can see it. You don't need to create it. You don't even need to look for it. You simply need to manage your state of being so that it's in a place where the path can find you.

In the introduction I mentioned a gut feeling. It's that gut feeling, present inside most of us, that tells us something isn't quite right and that life is supposed to be easier than it is. *This* is what that feeling is alluding to. You are living your life in opposition to the way your life is meant to be lived. Your life is meant to be a joyous, easy experience.

By not tuning into this guidance provided by your inner being, you are creating a life where struggle and worry become the norm, the norm that's been accepted as the standard way of living in most societies. This pattern of struggle, of settling for mediocre circumstances, is not only accepted, it's expected. Life is a struggle because we expect it to be so, because we try and effort our way through unwanted circumstances rather than co-creating with our inner being and feeling the ease we are meant to experience. The way out of unwanted situations or mediocrity isn't through action and effort, but through working with your inner being so that solutions to those problems present themselves to you. This is how you shift your life. This is the realization that will allow you to evolve to a new level of the human experience.

The Next Evolution in the Human Experience

Up to this point you may have used action and effort to make your way through life. Working hard. Striving for a pension and building income by getting good education and finding a high-income, stable job. This is the logical route for an action oriented, outer world-focused person. As you now know, however, you can't control outer world circumstances through external action; therefore this approach has no alternative but to be difficult, an approach that involves more time in an office and more time working, but wishing you could be doing something you really wanted.

The alternative is a transition from living your life in a state of doing, living your life from a state of being. We're human beings after all, not human doings.

When switching from a doing-based to a being-based approach to life, you go from living your life from a place of action and effort to a place of ease and allowance. Simply choose to feel good, follow the flow of inspiration and the intuitive nudges you receive, and let your desires come to you.

Your role on the physical plane of the human experience isn't to figure things out. Your role is simply to allow. The role of the physical you is to dream up desires, manage your attraction point, and follow your excitement. This will align you with those desires and allow them to manifest in the most beautiful ways possible, with the most perfect timing - a process where ease and effortlessness dominate.

You might be choosing to struggle because you believe achievement comes through action. This belief might come from the way in which you have been raised, from programming you may have picked up from your parents, or from observing those around you. In reality, achievement comes through vibrational alignment. Those who have a constant stream of success without effort, through what seems like sheer luck, aren't lucky. Whether they know it or not they are finding states of alignment and flow. They are allowing success to find them through the way they feel. They may seem happy due to their success when in fact, the opposite is the case - they are successful because they choose to be happy.

When you learn how to properly manage your frequency, the non-physical part of you makes things happen behind the scenes by creating synchronicities. You only need to take action when you feel inspired to do so, when it excites you, when you are guided by such a strong feeling that you can't *not* act. The impulse is so strong that the thought of ignoring it doesn't even feel like an option.

How does this impact the way you should live your life? You need to stop doing. Stop trying to work your way towards end goals you believe will make you happy. Prioritize how you feel above all else. Focus on feeling good first. This is what will allow those things you want to come to you.

Your feelings are your guide, like a GPS, attempting to direct you through your emotions. Ignore your emotions and you're literally ignoring guidance from your inner being, the part of you that has a much broader and more expansive viewpoint of your experience. By learning to trust and follow your guidance, you will allow yourself to be guided to your desires (or rather have them guided to you) as opposed to attempting to effort your way to their manifestation.

It is important to take note that there is a delay in manifestation. Lets call it a 'digestion period' or 'lag in the download'. When you initially begin to focus strictly on feeling good, it may take a bit of time before you begin to notice a shift in your reality. Some individuals see a shift right away while others may see a shift after four or five weeks. Your ability to create a shift is reflected in your ability to consistently control your state of being.

The True Power of Your Inner Being

One day in early 2014, Anik and I were sitting at the kitchen island discussing business ideas with the intention of figuring out how grow my coaching business and improve my marketing strategy. After an hour of chatting we felt like we hadn't made any progress and lacked any fresh ideas so we moved on to other things. A few hours later, Anik received an email from a mailing list, which she forwarded to me, mentioning that it was exactly what I needed. The video was from a very successful female with an extremely large internet following who specialized in online entrepreneurship. She also had a spiritual background and had hosted events with many of my favourite spiritual authors. I was blown away by the content in her video so I quickly subscribed to her channel.

The very next morning, while doing my morning practice, I watched nearly a dozen of her videos while on the elliptical. Her video content was exactly what I was looking for, but the story doesn't end there.

As I hopped off my elliptical I remember thinking to myself how beneficial it would be to have a chat with this woman, and that if there was a single person I would want to get some marketing tips from, it would be her. I was doubtful she would even respond to an email due to her large online following. Once I completed my morning routine I checked out her website and for some strange reason it looked vaguely familiar. A distant memory popped into my mind of my EFT trainer (who would be visiting the following weekend for another workshop) mentioning this person in the past and stating she knew her personally.

I opened Facebook, noticed my EFT trainer was online, and brought up the subject of the website and asked if she knew the person in these videos personally. She responded that yes, and not only had they recently had coffee, but the woman was signed up for the EFT course my trainer and I were hosting at my place the upcoming weekend!

I was going to have the opportunity to not only chat with her, but I'd also have the pleasure to host her, along with a dozen other amazing people, for three full days.

As you can see in this story, the universe had already arranged for this marketing expert to spend a few days in my home, before I knew I wanted to chat with her. Before I even knew she existed.

I could share many more synchronicities like this with you, but by far, the best way for you to truly understand the power of the universe is to learn how to get into a place where you are fully connected and experiencing it for yourself.

Up to this point in life you may have very little awareness of what is truly possible when fully tapping into the power of your inner being. Every day I express gratitude for my awareness and for the incredible synchronicities that occur in my life on a daily basis. What does existing in a state of truly aligned living look like? How do you know you've achieved the next evolution of the human experience? The following bulleted points outline the dominant traits that quickly become daily occurrences in your life.

» You frequently find yourself in states of flow and are living your life like a pro athlete who's in the zone, instinctively weaving and spinning around opponents in an almost supernatural way, you're flowing through life circumstances like nobody's business. You simply know what decisions to make, and where to turn. When a solution to a problem is required, the solution finds you.

» Synchronicities happen frequently and on an ongoing basis. You realize, without a shadow of doubt, higher universal forces are at work for you. You settle into knowing everything is always working out for you. You achieve a greater sense of inner peace than you ever believed was possible. Your level of trust in the way life is playing out is at an all time high.

» Joy is your dominant state. You wake up happy and excited for your day, just as you woke up happy and excited as a child.

» Clarity is prominent. Most decisions don't feel like decisions at all. You don't feel the need to rationalize your choices and you simply choose the path that feels best.

» You're enjoying life. This doesn't mean contrasting experiences or difficult moments won't occur. However, you know that by maintaining a good-feeling state and managing your attraction point, difficult situations somehow resolve themselves far easier than before.

PAINTING A NEW REALITY

THE BASIS OF YOUR life is freedom. You didn't choose to experience this reality as a victim of circumstances. You came into this reality fully knowing the true potential of what you could co-create alongside your inner being. Unfortunately, you may have forgotten who and what you really are and the true power of what you can achieve. You've been living your life disconnected from your inner being. Likely, it's felt like an uphill battle with more effort and struggle than was ever intended.

Although you may have been ignoring your inner being up to this point, it always has been and always will be by your side. Your inner being loves you. It wants you to be happy and it's waiting to begin working with you so it can deliver your greatest desires to you. Now that it knows you're finally aware of its presence, it's likely more excited than it ever has been. I hope you are too.

If I were to paint a picture of the new reality I am inviting you to experience, how would it look? I'd venture to say, it would probably look something like this:

You have the awareness that you can chose the way you feel in each and every moment, and make happiness a priority. Unlike a dog chasing its own tail, you no longer search for happiness in the material world, through various achievements or the validation of others. You realize that you have great power over your emotional state and you can actively choose to focus on reaching for the best feeling place possible, regardless of your circumstances. You recognize that living a reactionary life doesn't serve you. You're not a victim of your circumstances and those circumstances have no power over the way you feel.

You understand that manipulating circumstances to feel better is the backward way of living. The emotions you feel aren't meant to be a response to the situations in your life. The situations in your life are in fact responding to your thoughts and emotions. You understand you can't run away from a circumstance without shifting the thoughts and beliefs you hold, otherwise your reality will only reflect this circumstance back to you in a slightly different way. You're no longer trying to control and manipulate your circumstances in order to improve on the way you feel.

When you feel stuck or when unwanted situations occur, you go within. You question which part of you, which emotions or beliefs you hold, are responsible for attracting this circumstance.

You know that by tuning into the guidance of your inner being you can allow it to bring to you your greatest desires. Although you have great desires and aspirations, they are always second to the seeking of joy because in the end, joy is what you're after with all those desires and aspirations anyway. You understand that effort that isn't fun or doesn't excite you is overrated and is the old way of doing things.

Multiple times throughout the day you tune into your inner guidance and follow its lead in pursuing what feels best in each moment. You make your passion a priority. When intuitive nudges or synchronicities occur you give them a high level of attention. Even if your rational mind, fears, or beliefs step in and try to invalidate these nudges, you give them no attention. When your rational mind questions a course of action, you give the course of action the benefit of the doubt. When a word or image randomly pops into your mind, you don't ignore it. You spend little time planning your days and more of your time following your greatest excitement.

Life is a happy, joyful experience. You understand the key role your emotional state plays in this experience and you never ignore the way you feel. You process every negative emotion that surfaces so it can be fully released from your attraction point. If you've noticed that you've been harbouring a negative emotion for an extended period of time, you learn tools, or seek out someone who can help you to let it fully go. You realize that holding onto emotions weighs you down, pulls you out of your happy place, may block desires or attract unwanted situations, and may also impact your physical well-being in undesirable ways.

Because you've done a good job managing your emotional baggage you wake up each morning happy, excited, and anticipating what good things might happen next. You take comfort in the knowing that your inner being is there for you, guiding you and helping you along every step of your path. You understand that it has a much broader perspective of your reality and is much better suited to the task of making your dreams a reality. You hand over control to your inner being and only take action when you know it comes from an inspired place, free of any doubt. You feel the love coming from your inner being, the universe, and those around you. Because you are letting love in, you feel loved. Because you feel loved, the situations in your life reflect this love back to you. This makes you feel whole and complete, like nothing is missing in your life because you feel connected with the universe at such a deep level. You no longer have the desperate need to be in a relationship or to find your perfect mate because there is no longer a void needing to be filled. Because this void and the desperation have disappeared, it's easy for your inner being to deliver your ideal mate directly to your doorstep.

Challenging circumstances sometimes arise; however, you begin to trust that these are part of your path. Even though you may momentarily feel as though something has gone wrong, you reflect on these circumstances and allow them to play out without resisting them, eventually realizing that everything is always unfolding perfectly in your reality. This realization helps you move through the challenges at a much quicker pace and you understand that these situations are designed to bring you new awareness, to help you grow, and are part of the best possible path to your desires.

Ready to Experience the New Reality?

This picture I've painted of a new reality is fully achievable by anyone. It's an accurate representation of the way I live my life and it's the reality I'm hoping you'll reach for too. In the next section I've created practical steps to help you experience this new reality. These are the focus points and roadmap I use with all my clients.

Even though you may be worried about the amount of work involved and may be fearful of the level of complexity,

I assure you that anyone can do it. Don't let your ego make excuses or talk you out of it. Learn to use the power of joy so you can experience life the way we are meant to be living it. This way of living is so intrinsically natural, but because many of us have been disconnected for so long, ignoring our emotions, returning to this natural state does take some focus. With my clients, shifts often become evident after about four weeks and rarely do I need to work with anyone for more than eight. Regardless of the approach you take, every little bit helps. Every little step brings you closer to a reality where you're giving birth to new and miraculous experiences.

To those who are ready to commit and take that next step, the step that I believe is the next step in the evolution of our human experience, I offer my hearty congratulations. I applaud you for wanting more. I'm excited for every single person who reads this book, but especially for those who are willing to dive in and take action. You're about to discover a whole new way of experiencing life: A life of joy and bliss that I believe we are all truly meant to live.

PART 2
YOUR ROADMAP TO LIFE 2.0

Tools and Techniques for
Massive Transformation

SHIFTING TO A NEW REALITY

CALL ME CRAZY BUT I love to see people happy and succeeding.

When I decided to write this book my goal wasn't to become a best selling author or to make tons of money. My goal was to help you transform your life in the same way I have. The stories and concepts I've shared so far are indeed powerful, but you will need to put it into action to see for yourself. There is nothing I want more for you than the ability to experience the kind of joy and flow that I've found, and for you to succeed so that you, in turn, are co-creating with your inner being and living the life you really want to be living. I love knowing that you too will be inspiring others to make the journey to a better life as well.

With the beauty of self-publishing, new books by thousands of authors hit the theoretical bookshelves every day. Although these books are helping people all over the world learn, grow, and gain new understandings, many people lack the inspiration to take action. They read the book, and understand the concepts, but fail to take action on the lessons being taught therein.

In this section I'm sharing with you everything I do with my clients. As a coach I have an extremely high success rate; the formula I use works. What I'm sharing with you now is that formula. It includes powerful tools and techniques which, if fully applied, will change your life. What you choose to do with this information is in your hands. Maybe you're ok with the current circumstances in your life and feel like there's no need to take action. Or maybe you're an action taker, maybe you're tired of settling for the circumstances that aren't serving you and you want more out of life. Maybe you're ready to begin to harness the power of your inner being and shift your reality in ways you never thought possible.

With a little commitment and the application of the exercises that follow, you will easily achieve a more consistent state of joy. That joy will help you experience synchronicities similar to those I've mentioned in the previous chapters of this book. Your only focus in applying this information is in reaching for higher and higher levels of joy. Measure your success only by the way you feel and not by the manifestations of the synchronicities or desires you may want to experience. By reaching for, and achieving, a state of unconditional joy you will feel happier, healthier, and you'll be shifting your attraction point in a way that will undoubtedly get you more of what you want.

Don't just seek joy. Allow it to become the fuel that powers your existence.

Shifting to a new reality may take you days, weeks, months, or even years. The length of time doesn't matter. Some people immediately plough through the tasks in front of them. They buy the right resources or hire the right people to get the job done as quickly as possible. Others prefer to take their time and enjoy the ride. It took me almost a decade, but mind you, I didn't have the same direction or information I'm providing you. I had to figure it out on my own. Don't compare your experiences and your approach to applying this material with anyone else. Your approach to shifting your inner world is as unique to you as the life you've lived and the experiences you've collected along the way.

Ready to get started? Here are a few key points before you get going.

1. Commit.

If I had to pick out one key contributing factor to the degree of success I witness a client experience, it would be their level of commitment. If you want results, as with anything else in life, you need to commit to the process. Taking the time to clear the emotional baggage you've collected may take a few weeks, or even months. This is a very small amount of time to dedicate to a process that will have lifelong benefits. The circumstances around you may shift slowly at first, and may not even seem to be noticeable right away. On the other hand, you might experience huge, immediate shifts that are extremely apparent. If you're properly clearing out your inbox and creating positive momentum as explained in the pages that follow, you will see significant shifts. Like going to the gym or dedicating yourself to other goals, your level of commitment will determine your level of success. There is no magic pill, but in my experience, a deep commitment is a definite precursor to success. When I work with a committed client who is consistent with their daily practice and doing a good job of clearing their negative emotions, I often see shifts within a few weeks.

2. Join Shift Club

If someone wants to experience massive success in the transformation of their body, they hire a personal trainer. If they want massive success with regard to their inner transformation, they come to Shift Club. I've created a powerful online community to assist you in applying the teachings in this book. It contains a message board, guided meditation audios, worksheets, instructional videos, and follow-along EFT tapping videos. As a member, you get my personal support and can reach out to me with questions. I highly recommend joining if you're serious about applying the teachings in this book. More details can be found online at: *http://discoverthepowerofjoy.com/shiftclub*

> # #SHIFTCLUB

3. Seek Joy

If you picked up this book, odds are you're looking for something. It may be that perfect relationship, more money, clarity regarding your life purpose, more inner peace, or something completely different. If your goal is to become a master at manifestation, you need to practise detaching from your desires. Put them aside for the length of time you're committing to your shift and make the seeking of joy your only focus. Seek joy not for the purpose of manifesting your desires, but for the purpose of seeing how much joy you can achieve. Manifestations will occur with much more ease once you're consistently achieving states of flow.

4. You're Running a Marathon, Not a Race

Consistency is critical. Are you looking to experience big shifts and synchronicities and feeling impatient for them to show up? Expect them, but don't allow an initial lack of their presence to be an indicator of your progress. There's always a gestation period between the time of your finding the feeling of joy, and the actual manifestation of what you're experiencing in the physical. Once you start achieving high states of joy, work on holding those states. Initially, most individuals hit new highs, but are unable to maintain these states for any period of time. While this is a sign of progress, note that bouncing between high and low points is not enough to create the consistent state of flow you're looking to achieve. Stay patient and keep up the pace. By following the plan I've outlined below, you can rest assured those big shifts are right around the corner.

Three Parts to a Shift

The formula I'm outlining for you is the same formula I use with my clients. It doesn't matter if they come to me for assistance with relationships, career, life purpose, money, anxiety, inner peace, or anything else for that matter. It's all the same work.

The first part is identifying the unwanted beliefs and emotions in your attraction point. These are the things you've collected over the course of your life that are pulling you out of your natural state of joy and disconnecting you from your inner being. These are the same things that also keep you stuck in unwanted situations or prevent you from manifesting certain desires.

How do you identify the unwanted aspects in your attraction point? You look at the unwanted aspects in your reality and trace them back to how you think and feel using probing questions. For example, do you have multiple circumstances going on that make you feel powerless? Maybe you never have enough money and are in a relationship where you feel controlled.

If so, odds are your attraction point contains powerlessness. This identification process is fully explained in the next few chapters, along with step-by-step directions on how to do it. In these chapters you'll learn specific probing questions for emotions. You'll learn different probing questions for beliefs. We'll also look at how you can use your physical body and any existing dis-ease to identify what negative beliefs and emotions you may be storing in your attraction point.

Once you've completed the identification work you'll then want to move on to the second, and in my opinion, the more exciting part - the clearing work.

It's great to have identified the detrimental emotions present in your attraction point, however nothing will shift until you let these go. The second part of the formula is clearing the emotions and beliefs you have identified. When working with clients, this is the majority of the work and, when done successfully, this is the work that will create the most noticeable impact on the way you feel and on the circumstances in your life.

In the following chapters I'll explain a few different clearing techniques, as well as my go-to tool: Emotional Freedom Technique (or Tapping). I'm a big fan of EFT, which is why I use it frequently with my clients as well as in my online support community.

The third and final part is learning how to create positive momentum. This process focuses on directing your thought patterns and the way you feel early in the day, so you can set the tone for how your day will play out. This part can be done in parallel to the identification and clearing work.

How Should You Apply This Formula?

When I set out to work with clients we usually complete eight sessions over an eight-week period. In our first session, we establish a morning practice that the client can use on a daily basis to create positive momentum. In that same session we also do the identification work (parts one and three of the three-part formula). The following seven sessions are almost all clearing work using EFT in our weekly meetings while the client continues to apply their morning practice every day.

If you're doing this work on your own, you can start with either the morning momentum or the identification and clearing work. Both of these can be done concurrently, however I suggest starting with one part at a time. If you have lots of free time in the morning, starting with a few weeks of positive morning momentum may work best. If you're busy in the morning but have lots of free time in the evening, start with identification and clearing. There is no best way to apply the formula.

When explaining this work to others, the topic of clearing emotions is often met with a look of fear. For reasons I have yet to figure out, as if it were a monster hiding in a closet, most people have come to be afraid of their emotional baggage. I can assure you there is nothing to fear. Your emotions can't hurt you in any way. By turning around and facing them you'll realize how powerful you truly are. After clearing significant emotional baggage you'll be amazed at how much lighter you feel. You may notice shifts in physical symptoms that have lasted for years, and you may even immediately notice major shifts in other aspects of your life.

One of my more recent clients, Kara, was a young woman looking to establish a hypnotherapy practice. Kara unknowingly had emotions in her attraction point that made it a struggle to consistently attract new clients. After our fourth session, which was focused on clearing emotions around self-worth and fear of failure, she sent me an email with the following message, which clearly demonstrates the shifts that can occur.

Hi Nick, I wanted to give you a brief update on my progress. Whatever we worked on in our last session (the general negativity and fear of failure) made the biggest impact yet. Remember how I wanted to experience a manifestation out of the blue? Well here is what happened and it will probably blow your mind. That exact day I had not 1 but 2 old clients ask for a session either for themselves, or for a friend. That night I went into work and a very shy girl I was training was drawn to conversation with me. I revealed I was a hypnotherapist and she asked for a session. The next day in a taxicab to the airport the driver and I started having more than just small talk. We talked about travel and relationships and somehow got into hardships and emotions. Never once did I mention I was a hypnotherapist. He kept saying that there was something different about me and asked what I did. I told him I was a hypnotherapist and he started crying! He shared how it was difficult to break up with his girlfriend and mentioned that their anniversary is the same day as the day in his favourite movie *Back to the Future*. Not only is *Back to the Future* my all-time favourite movie but it has also been an ongoing synchronicity for me for the past 2 months. I had the chills!

Letting go of those specific emotions, which she likely held since childhood created the necessary shift that landed Kara a handful of clients within almost twenty-four hours of her session, while also throwing in a fun bit of synchronicity. Further in this chapter we'll explore various clearing methods so you can determine which approach is best suited for you.

Summary of Tools and Techniques

Here's your roadmap with the steps and processes you'll be going through in this section.

Part 1 – Attraction Point Identification

Identify what you may be holding in your attraction point in each of three areas:

1. Emotions

2. Beliefs

3. Physical Symptoms

Part 2 – Clearing Tools

Once you've identified the emotions, beliefs, and physical symptoms you hold, the next step is to let them go, using the following techniques:

1. Emotional Freedom Technique

2. Time Line Therapy

3. Meditation

4. Positive Daily Practice

Part 3 – Creating Positive Momentum

Create positive momentum and learn to maintain thought patterns that will help you more easily achieve and maintain states of joy through:

1. Positive Daily Practice

2. Powerful Processes

   a. Automatic Writing

   b. Focus Wheel

   c. Sacred Container

   d. Positive Aspects List

   e. Polarity Processing

ATTRACTION POINT ANALYSIS - DIGGING INTO YOUR EMOTIONS

A COUPLE OF YEARS ago I was out for a night on the town with a small group of friends. David, one of my closest friends, asked me for help; he felt stuck. He explained to me how he had completely lost all his motivation at work and could barely get himself out of bed and didn't know what to do. I asked David to identify one thing he would change that would improve his situation. He responded: his financial situation.

I asked him how his financial situation currently made him feel. "Powerless," he said.

Next, I had David focus on his last significant relationship. I asked him what the worst part was about that relationship. After a few seconds of reflecting he said that communication was the biggest issue. His former girlfriend always had to win every argument and have the last word. She never wanted to do what he wanted. They always hung out with her friends and never hung out with his. She made all the decisions when they were together and would never listen to him. Again, I asked how this situation made him feel. His answer once again was "powerless."

I then took David into other past significant relationships and other past events in his life. As I asked what emotion each event was delivering to him, the theme of powerlessness became apparent. Powerlessness was a dominant theme throughout David's entire life. Sitting squarely in his attraction point this dominant negative emotion was impacting both his relationships and his finances.

I also took David all the way back to childhood where the seeds of dominant negative emotions are most often planted. I asked David if he could recall any themes of powerlessness as a child. David explained to me that he was the youngest of three children. He remembered how nobody ever wanted to do what he wanted to do. He always had to follow his older siblings around, playing the games they wanted to play, always doing what they wanted to do, never what he wanted.

It was apparent that since his childhood David was holding a dominant negative emotion of powerlessness.

Right there in the pub we followed up our digging by doing some emotional clearing work using tapping on the emotions of powerlessness and related aspects. An hour later, the waitress brought the bills for everyone at our table - all but David's. She forgot his. She said she was tired, the computers were already being shut down and she didn't want to go back to print another bill. David's drinks were on the house! Within the next few months, not only did David find a better, higher paying job, he also found himself in a new long-term relationship, a very different relationship with no hint of the same powerlessness that had haunted him in the past.

David's story demonstrates how we often carry emotions of which we are unaware. In my experience, most of us carry a small number of these dominant negative emotions - often picked up during childhood or through traumatic events - that continually impact the circumstances in our lives.

Releasing a dominant negative emotion from your attraction point almost always creates a big shift. Most people have been hanging on to certain emotions for so long they don't even realize they are present. All negative emotions, even those you've had since birth, can be cleared. The length of time you've been hanging on to an emotion has no impact on the amount of work required to clear it. Negative emotions are not part of you. They aren't who you are.

Have you ever taken the time to notice how often negative emotions surface in your life? If you reflect on past experiences and the emotions that go along with them, are you noticing a pattern?

Identifying Your Dominant Negative Emotions

When looking for the root cause of a bug in a computer system, developers often need to reverse engineer the code. What does this mean exactly? You start with the end product (the running program) and move your way down to its core, the computer code, based on the program's behaviour. In a nutshell, you analyze the behaviour before going into the guts of the system.

In order to determine your dominant negative emotion, as well as any other emotion in your attraction point, you can follow the same process and reverse engineer your reality. You now know that your outer world experiences are a reflection of your state of being. Every situation you attract is based on the beliefs and emotions you're storing in your attraction point. So how do you reverse engineer your reality? Simple. You look at past experiences that bring up negative emotions and identify the two or three dominant emotions that each circumstance brings up. You can do this using this simple probing question:

"How does this circumstance or situation make me feel?"

When looking at past circumstances and asking this question, you'll likely begin to notice that the same few emotions continually surface for most of those past circumstances. This won't be the case for everyone, but in my experience approximately 80% to 85% of the people I work with are able to identify dominant negative emotions through this process.

Take Action

Are you ready to identify your dominant negative emotions? Depending on your level of self-awareness, you might already have an idea what emotions are there - or you might be very surprised! For this exercise you'll want to find a quiet space where distractions will be kept to a minimum. Give yourself at least a half hour.

In order to continue you'll need a pen and paper or a journal. Although it isn't absolutely necessary, I like to suggest keeping a journal, so all your thoughts are in one place. Use your journal for your morning gratitude work and evening reflection (to be discussed in an upcoming section). Your journal will assist you in gaining valuable realizations about yourself and the way your circumstances impact the way you feel.

In Shift Club you can also find a worksheet to support you through this exercise.

> #SHIFTCLUB

Ready to take action and get shifting? Log in to Shift Club and download the worksheet titled *Digging into Emotions*. *http://discoverthepowerofjoy.com/shiftclub*

Open your journal to a new page. Begin by identifying the situations in your life that would have brought up (and may still bring up) strong emotions. This list should contain circumstances such as:

» Traumatic events (anything from being embarrassed at school to car accidents to social faux pas and beyond)

» Issues from past significant relationships

» Difficult relationships with your parents, siblings, and other family members

» Problems or limitations related to financial situation

» Unwanted situations around your career or job situation

» The biggest stresses in your life

» Situations around physical health, chronic pain, and body image

» Anything else that comes to mind that has a significant emotional charge.

Once your list is complete, in regard to each point on the list, ask the probing question: **"How does this situation or circumstance make me feel?"**. Write down the top one or two negative emotions that surface next to each item. Also take note of the negative emotions that surface most frequently for you on a daily basis and add them to the bottom of your list.

The following list of negative emotions may be used as a reference.

» Anger	» Frustration
» Sadness	» Pressured
» Fear	» Unsupported
» Hurt	» Hopelessness
» Guilt	» Overwhelm
» Powerlessness	» Confusion
» Unworthiness	» Rejection
» Helplessness	» Shame

Once your list is complete, count the frequency of each emotion you've identified. If a few emotions are surfacing much more frequently than others, odds are you've identified a dominant negative emotion. If you can trace this emotion back to a childhood situation, you've most definitely identified a dominant negative emotion.

If you've managed to identify one or more dominant negative emotions you'll want to use these emotions as a starting point for your clearing work. Clearing these emotions should create a significant and immediate shift in your life. If you were unable to identify a dominant negative emotion, start your clearing work with whatever emotions surface most frequently for you in your daily life.

The Big Six Emotions

My in-depth, one-on-one work with clients has clearly shown that there are certain repressed emotions that come up more frequently than others. Below, are what I call the Big Six. If you feel stuck or unable to break free from specific circumstances in your life, it's possible one of these may be the cause.

Are you able to identify which of the following fears and emotions might be currently impacting your life?

1. Fear of Failure

Fear of failure is one of the less obvious fears that keep people stuck, but it is nonetheless quite common. Growing up, did you have family members who constantly criticized you? Were your parents always focused on your mistakes and never satisfied by your performance? Were you often humiliated as a child? Fear of failure often goes hand in hand with low self-esteem and feelings of not being good enough. Fear of failure doesn't only apply to work scenarios, it also manifests in other aspects of life such as relationships. Have you experienced major heartbreak after a sudden and unexpected end to a relationship? At a subconscious level this can create a self-sabotaging pattern that prevents you from stepping into future serious relationships. The fear of suffering yet another major heartbreak or potential blow to the ego may be so strong that you'd rather not take the risk and so you sabotage your relationships.

The following symptoms may indicate of a fear of failure:

- » A tendency towards perfectionism
- » Frequent procrastination
- » A lack of motivation or difficulty finishing projects
- » Feelings of low self-worth
- » Suffering from anxiety
- » Having grown up in an environment of criticism

If you suffer from a fear of failure, it most likely isn't the failure itself that you fear but the consequences that go along with it. If you're stuck in a particular situation, use the probing question: "What's the worst thing that could happen?" For example, if you noticed a theme of self-sabotaging in relationships, try asking: "If I was to develop a serious relationship, would be the worst thing that could happen, and how would that make me feel?" If a specific scenario and emotion come up, work on clearing it from your attraction point through one of the methods explained further on in this section.

2. Fear of Change

The fear of change is often an undetected fear that flies under the radar. Are there specific things you'd like to change in your life, but you're afraid of what may go along with these changes? Major life changes in career, relationship, or physical location may stir up these hidden fears. It's not uncommon to remain in a career or relationship that may not be serving you because you're afraid that by leaving you'll end up in a less favourable position.

One of the subtle, yet common fears that keeps people stuck in a state of struggle, is the fear that surrounds changes to perceived identity. Amber was a client who came to me looking for assistance in her struggle to lose weight. I asked Amber: "If you were to reach your target weight, what would be the absolute worst thing that would occur as a result?" After pausing for a few seconds, her eyes grew wide as she answered: "I don't know what I'd do with myself." She realized something that had never occurred to her: losing weight was her life! Her weight loss battle had become her top hobby as she studied nutrition, read weight loss magazines, and poured over countless blogs.

Without her weight loss struggle, who would Amber be? She had made losing weight part of her identity. Subconsciously, her weight loss battle had become a part of who she was.

Her identity was the root cause of why she was struggling to lose weight. It induced self-sabotaging behaviours because even though she consciously wanted to lose the weight, subconsciously, it wasn't an option. The fear of who she would become without this struggle was keeping her stuck.

The following symptoms may indicate a fear of change:

» Feeling like you're settling in specific situations in life such as career or relationship - you know you could do better, but you'd rather play it safe than risk finding yourself in a less favourable situation

» Not taking action on a desire because of how others may react to your decision

» Ignoring the fact that your heart is calling you in a certain direction because you're uncertain as to how it will all play out

» A focus on taking the path that creates the most stability, not on the path that creates the most excitement

3. Feeling "Not Good Enough"

Zack was a memorable client. A scientist living in Europe, he was suffering from feelings of not being good enough. Growing up, Zack was extremely intelligent and excelled in school, earning top marks with very little effort. He went on to an Ivy League college and took up a prominent position in the research department of a leading edge company. You would think some-one with such outstanding career and academic success would be proud of his accomplishments. Zack, however, suffered from feelings of not being good enough. Even though he excelled in some areas of his life, he was less successful in others. Growing up he was always picked last in gym class. His social skills were sub par and he always found himself alone at dances and proms. He had highly critical parents who were always pushing him to do better. These experiences contributed to the cultivation of Zack's feeling of not being good enough. Once the emotion had settled into his inner inbox, it felt permanent. He couldn't shake it. Because the emotion was now part of his attraction point, it was negatively impacting every area of his life. He was attracting relationships that made him feel like he wasn't good enough and found himself working for individuals who were always criticizing his work and treating him poorly.

The following symptoms may indicate a fear of not being good enough:

»   Being involved in relationships with people who treat you poorly or constantly put you down

»   Feeling criticized or judged.

»   A history of being frequently criticized or judged by a family member

»   A history of being frequently picked on in school

»   Feeling like you just don't fit in much of the time

»   A tendency for perfectionism

4. Feeling Powerless

Powerlessness is a crippling emotion that most people don't realize they are carrying. In fact, I see strong feelings of powerlessness in almost half my clients. The feeling of powerlessness can get a foothold in a variety of situations at various stages throughout life. When he was a child, my client Eric's brother tied him to a tree, and left him alone, stranded and helpless. As it turns out, Eric was only left alone for 15 minutes but the fear and trauma he experienced during that time caused him to feel a sense of powerlessness that permeated his existence throughout his life until together, we worked to free him of that feeling.

Do you suffer from a poor financial situation? Do you have relationships with loved ones or co-workers wherein you feel like you're not being heard? Do you suffer from chronic lower back problems? These are all common symptoms that you have a sense of powerlessness in your attraction point.

Feelings of lack of control go hand-in-hand with powerlessness. Although not identical, they carry the same symptoms and have similar impact on your attraction point. Karen, an acquaintance I met online, was looking for advice with regard to a chronic lower back issue. When I asked her how she hurt her back, she responded it wasn't one particular event and that it had developed over time. She thought it might have been due to one of the five minor car accidents she had experienced over the previous year and a half. Karen wasn't a bad driver and most of these accidents weren't her fault. Based on the fact that she was suffering from chronic lower back pain and feelings of lack of control due to the frequent accidents, I suspected she was hanging on to major feelings of powerlessness. I asked her to recall any major events in her life in the months prior to her first accident. I wanted to know what trauma could have occurred that would have made her feel powerless.

She shared with me that she had been hosting a student from another country. The exchange student suffered from serious depression and, while in Karen's care, had attempted to take her life. Fortunately, the student is still alive. Unfortunately for Karen, the student's parents refused to take her back. Karen felt stuck, and uncertain as to what to do about the situation. She felt completely powerless and unable to find the help she needed. Eventually the situation resolved itself. Due to the trauma related to this situation, Karen ended up with major emotions of powerlessness and a lack of control in her attraction point.

The following symptoms may indicate a feeling of powerlessness or lack of control:

» Suffering from chronic lower back pain

» A strong urge to want to control the circumstances in your life

» A fear of flying

» Experiencing frequent car accidents

» Having a hard time getting ahead financially – feeling like you can't do anything you want because you lack money

» Feeling like you're not being heard - your kids, or coworkers, refusing to listen to you

» Feeling stuck in unwanted situations in your life, with no foreseeable way out

5. Feeling Unworthy

Lack of self-worth is another commonly repressed negative emotion. Feeling unworthy is frequently associated with negative emotions including sadness, guilt, shame, and hopelessness. Did you suffer from abuse or did family members treat you as though you had no value, or nothing to contribute? Did anyone ever make you feel like you weren't good enough? Do you suffer from body image issues? These are just a few of the many ways that you could establish feelings of low self-worth. It's also been my experience that anxiety and depression sufferers have a tendency to carry emotions of low self-worth.

The following symptoms may indicate a feeling of low self-worth:

» Attracting relationships in which your partner insults you or treats you with little regard

» Experiencing a poor body image

» Suffering from anxiety or depression

» Having racing thoughts and worries about how others will judge or criticize you

» Being a perfectionist

» Having a hard time speaking up or being assertive

6. Feeling Unsafe

Fears around a lack of safety can keep you stuck in a number of circumstances in life. It's not uncommon to see people unknowingly self-sabotage relationships or finances because of safety issues. Jenna, one of my early clients, came to me because she recognized a self-sabotaging behaviour with regard to her business. Jenna was a brilliant entrepreneur who would always find ways to mess things up, just as she was poised on the verge of major success. As a general rule, she rarely made mistakes and only seemed to make them—big ones—when significant financial losses were a potential result.

After a little digging, Jenna shared with me that at the tender age of ten, she suffered the loss of her father. Even though she had done significant emotional work around the passing of her father, this flagged my suspicion. She explained that her father was a businessman and the family had been very wealthy. Her dad had invested all of the family fortune on what he anticipated to be a sure shot deal. He was wrong. The deal failed and the family lost their entire fortune. Jenna's father, heartbroken from the incident, developed post-traumatic stress and suddenly passed away as the result of a heart attack.

The trauma from this event caused Jenna's subconscious mind, wanting to keep her safe, to flag money as a threat to safety. It blamed wealth for the death of her father. At this moment, outside of Jenna's awareness, a self-sabotaging behaviour was born.

Significant traumas, such as a death in the family, aren't the only sources of financial self-sabotage. I've seen all kinds of safety issues around money with clients. Linda, a businesswoman who came to me because her five-figure monthly income had dwindled to almost nothing over the course of a year, wanted to know the root cause of her financial problem. The answer very quickly became apparent. She was unhappy with the way her husband was spending money. Her husband was an intimidating man and Linda was subconsciously sabotaging her income so as not to have to deal with his demands. She hadn't realized that she had unwittingly cut off the family income source so that she wouldn't have to deal with the real problem: the discomfort with the way her husband spent money.

Relationships can feel unsafe for those of us who have experienced past relationship problems or grown up witnessing our parents in less than ideal relationships. Have you ever experienced a relationship where trust, control, or emotional or physical abuse may have been issues? Investigate any fears you hold around past relationships that may be preventing you from feeling comfortable about developing new relationships in the present. Once again, try asking the probing question: "If I was in a relationship, what would be the absolute worst thing that could happen?" This will help you find any fears around safety that could be holding you back.

The following symptoms may indicate a feeling of being unsafe:

» Self-sabotaging behaviours in your relationships, career, or financial situations

» Relationships always ending within the same general time frame

» Fears of moving forward in aspects of your life

ATTRACTION POINT ANALYSIS –
DIGGING INTO YOUR BELIEFS

In one of our previous stories, David, who had remained a victim of powerlessness for most of his life, was completely unaware that he was carrying the burden of this disabling emotion. Most people are unaware not only of the fact that they are carrying emotional baggage that is impacting their lives, but also of the very foundational beliefs they hold at the core of who they are.

Often, when discussing my current work with old friends they comment on how this new career - which consists of doing mental and emotional work with clients - is very different than what I used to do, debugging and programming computers. The truth is, working with people on the mental and emotional levels to help them shift their attraction point or curb unwanted behaviors is actually amazingly *similar* to troubleshooting or debugging a computer.

At the time of birth, like brand new computers, we are completely free from any programming. In the case of the computers, other than the operating system required for basic functionality, no software is installed. When it comes to us humans, our minds, new and fresh at our time of birth, are also free of the 'software' of emotional baggage and the beliefs that are responsible for our behaviour.

As we grow older and observe the world around us, we learn what is safe and what may be unsafe. We form our beliefs: some of which serve us, and others that hold us back. Like the programs we add to our computers to make them more efficient and productive, the 'programs' we collect in our minds are 'installed' in the hopes of bettering our lives.

Our behaviours, both wanted and unwanted, are rooted in these programs that keep running constantly in our minds. One of the responsibilities of our subconscious minds is to keep us safe. Although they mostly do a great job in this role, these subconscious protectors can sometimes experience bugs and programming glitches, just like computers.

Take Olivia for example.

At a young age Olivia had fallen madly in love with someone who became her high school sweetheart. Under the impression she had found her one true love, she was already planning her dream wedding in her mind. Unfortunately, in her senior year, Olivia was blindsided. She found out that her one true love had been cheating on her. This traumatic event brought on a great deal of hurt and emotional pain. It also did something that would impact Olivia's future relationships for a very long time.

In Olivia's case, the trauma experienced around the event of her boyfriend cheating on her was responsible for installing an unwanted program in her operating system. Because the trauma was unexpected, and painful, her subconscious mind developed a belief that falling in loving and being in a relationship was a threat to her safety. From this point forward, each and every relationship in which Olivia found herself would go drastically wrong. Relationships would begin to fall apart within a few months, just as it seemed they were about to get serious. Unaware that her subconscious mind was holding on to a belief that relationships were unsafe, she would unknowingly sabotage each of the relationships, in spite of the fact that they had actually been going very well.

Within less than four sessions we identified the root programming, cleared the emotional pain from the traumatic experience, and released the subconscious belief responsible for the self-sabotaging behaviour. Olivia's experience is not uncommon. In fact, I see this type of belief frequently impacting individuals, both in relationships and in their finances – the two areas where people seem to struggle most.

Unwanted beliefs and fears come in all shapes and sizes. Many people hold damaging beliefs such as, "I'm not worthy" or, "I'm unlovable" or, "I have to be perfect" as part of their attraction point. They may also harbor fears of not being good enough, or of being hurt. These unwanted beliefs, along with many others, undoubtedly have a profound negative impart on their life experiences.

You might pick up strongly rooted beliefs through repetition, especially as a child, repeatedly being told that you're not strong enough or that you're not as good as your older brother or sister. Or perhaps you were told that you always needed help or could never get it right. My clients with critical and judgemental parents heard these messages and suffered from feelings of not being good enough and experienced low self-worth.

Do you feel the need to be perfect? Do you believe the habit of seeking perfection is something that you were born with, or that developed over time? Those with perfectionistic tendencies have often grown up feeling the need to prove something. They may have felt inferior to other family members, seeking perfection in order to be noticed or to feel loved. They may have also been bullied and therefore seek to do everything "right" to avoid being picked on. Perfectionists also frequently suffer from chronic neck and shoulder pains due to the pressure they put on themselves. Those who developed perfectionistic tendencies at a young age maintain this pattern of perfectionism as they grow older. It becomes a subconscious, habitual behaviour they can non longer control.

Believing you are unsafe in a variety of situations can develop through repetition as well. If you've been mentally or physically abused in a relationship, fears around safety will likely become rooted. Situations like this promote the following beliefs: that it's not safe to be in a relationship, that you can't do what you want, or perhaps that you'll be controlled or need to compromise aspects of your life. All of these fears and negative beliefs impact the way you live. Regardless of how long these fears or beliefs have been present, they can always be cleared. Remember, like a virus in a computer, it was picked up at a specific point in time and in the same way a virus can be deleted from a computer, these beliefs can also be removed from your mind.

Identifying Your Beliefs

In order to help identify the beliefs you are holding, let's take a look at a few different probing questions. These questions can help you identify what may be stopping you from developing a perfect relationship, or experiencing success in your business or financial matters. These questions can also be used to find clarity with regard to any other circumstance that leaves you feeling stuck in your life. When it comes to the probing questions around emotions, you want to look at specific situations and ask how these situations make you feel. You want to find out what beliefs exist around a situation as well as what emotions could possibly be attached to them. You can do this using the following three probing questions:

1. If a desired outcome were to come true - if my goals were to be achieved - what would be the absolute worst thing that could happen?

2. In what ways would achieving this goal or desire make me feel unsafe?

3. In what ways am I benefiting from *not* achieving this goal?

Let's use weight loss as an example to illustrate the digging process, using these probing questions. These are all real answers given to me by past clients.

Situation: I'm overweight and want to lose 50 pounds, but no matter how hard I try, I just can't lose the weight.

Question 1: If I could achieve my ideal weight, what would be the worst thing that could happen?
Answer: My clothes would no longer fit me and I don't have the money to buy new ones. It makes me uncomfortable to be

tne centre of attention and if I lose weight people will notice and comment about it and I will feel judged.

Question 2: In what ways would achieving this goal or desire make me feel unsafe?
Answer: Everyone in my entire family, including my parents and siblings, has always been overweight. My brother makes fun of skinny people. If I lose my weight then I'll become the black sheep of the family. They may treat me differently. They might pick on me. They will judge me and maybe even stop loving me.

Question 3: In what ways am I benefiting from not achieving this goal?
Answer: By remaining overweight I don't have to worry about attracting attention from men, which makes me uncomfortable. I don't have to worry about eating things I know I shouldn't be eating.

When looking at these answers, it's clear how these beliefs can be responsible for weight loss struggles. Using these probing questions in any circumstance where you feel stuck often sheds light on thought patterns you may not be aware that you have. These can be especially helpful if you're struggling to attract or remain in relationships as there are often limiting beliefs around safety or compromise.

Your beliefs also have a strong tie to your emotional state. Gaining the awareness that you have a belief is sometimes enough to let it go. Other times, you may need to work on releasing the negative emotions tied to the belief.

If you'd like to identify the emotions tied to a specific belief, try asking how having that belief in regard to a situation makes you feel. Once again, using the weight loss example, you would follow up like this:

Belief: If I lose weight I want to lose, I would be the only skinny person in my family and they might make fun of me. I would be the black sheep of the family.

Probing question: How would this make me feel?

Answer: Sad and lonely.

Take Action

The purpose of this exercise is to help you identify any subconscious beliefs that could be holding you back in specific areas of your life. Once again, you'll want to find a quiet space where distractions will be kept to a minimum and give yourself at least a half hour to complete this exercise. You'll also need a pen and paper or a journal.

Start this exercise by opening up your journal to a new page, and begin by identifying the specific situations in your life where you feel stuck. In response to each situation, identify your true desired outcome in the related area of your life. For example, your list might look something like this:

» Situation: I never have any extra money to do the things I want to do.

» Desired Outcome: To manifest a large sum of money.

» Situation: I feel like I am always going to be single because my relationships never last very long.

» Desired Outcome: To manifest a lasting, loving relationship.

» Situation: I'm so tired of being overweight.

» Desired Outcome: To achieve my ideal weight.

Once you've completed your list, ask the following questions in relation to each of the circumstances you've outlined. Some of your answers may be obvious, while others could take you completely by surprise.

1. If my desired outcome were to come true - if my goals were to be achieved - what would be the absolute worst thing that could happen?

2. In what ways would achieving this goal or desire make me feel unsafe?

3. In what ways am I benefiting from *not* achieving this goal?

Once you've identified the emotions around these beliefs, your next step will be to work on clearing them. As with beliefs, sometimes gaining the awareness that these emotions exist is enough to create a shift. Other times, you'll want to use the clearing tools we'll be discussing later in this section.

| #SHIFTCLUB | Ready to take action and get shifting? Log in to Shift Club and download the worksheet titled **Busting Through Beliefs**. *http://discoverthepowerofjoy.com/shiftclub* |

ATTRACTION POINT ANALYSIS –
WHAT'S MY BODY TELLING ME?

ONE OF MY FAVOURITE (and most mind blowing) ways to identify if negative emotions and beliefs are present is by noticing an individual's physical body symptomology. Negative emotions can surface as ailments in the physical body. Louise Hay was the one of the first contemporary authors to document the link between emotions and physical well-being in her popular book *Heal Your Body*. I've personally seen people experience immediate shifts in chronic pain such as migraines, neck and back pains, and uncomfortable stomach issues simply by releasing negative emotions. The following story is about one of my clients, Lisa, who was off work due to panic attacks.

Lisa booked a private one-on-one EFT session with me because she had been off work for over a month due to panic-inducing feelings of overwhelm at the office. She was not sleeping well, had chronic pain (diagnosed as fibromyalgia), and near constant migraines, and wanted to know if I could help her resolve these issues.

Lisa and I began exploring the potential root cause of her issues. She shared how her young son was admitted to the hospital due to a condition requiring surgery approximately 18 months prior. Although the surgery was successful and life was back to normal, this was a traumatic event for Lisa. I asked her how she felt when reflecting on the event and her reply was, "helpless."

I then proceeded to ask Lisa about the last few months at the office just before her absenteeism became an issue. She stated that she had recently moved to a position in a different department and her new job included tasks that she didn't enjoy, but had to do. As a result of this situation, she began to experience feelings of helplessness.

These tasks and the related feelings of helplessness would normally be inconsequential for most. For Lisa, however, the situation was enough to push her over the edge emotionally, resulting in panic attacks and an inability to work. Why? Lisa was still holding on to unprocessed emotions from the traumatic event of her son's surgery. Those buried feelings of helplessness, which were no longer present at a conscious level, were still sitting in her inner inbox. They resurfaced causing her to experience feelings of overwhelm, panic, and insomnia.

I guided Lisa through a tapping process that helped her let go of the helplessness and other stuck emotions surrounding her past trauma. By the end of our session, Lisa felt lighter. She said that it felt like a huge invisible weight had been lifted off her shoulders.

When I followed up with her a few days later, she informed me that she was feeling much more grounded. Lisa's feelings of panic had disappeared, she was sleeping better, and her doctor had set a return to work date for her. Lisa returned for two more follow up sessions where other issues were addressed. These sessions allowed Lisa to address other emotions she had been carrying and she almost immediately saw drastic shifts in joint swelling and fibromyalgia to the point where she could now wear her wedding ring for the first time in over twelve months. After a fourth session she was excited to share that she was free from physical pain for the first time in over three years.

Lisa's situation is not uncommon. Unprocessed emotions - even if they are outside our conscious awareness - impact the way we feel, as well as our state of wellness, to varying degrees. They can also have a direct impact on our physical bodies..

Digging Deeper

For a number of years, I used *Heal Your Body* to link my physical symptoms to what may be going on in my attraction point. I recently discovered that there are newer books with an even greater level of detail. My favorite such reference book is *Metaphysical Anatomy*, by Evette Rose (EvetteRose.com). The book details which physical symptoms might be linked to which unprocessed emotions, and it is so uncannily accurate that it routinely blows my clients' minds. When I first purchased her book, I made a list of a half dozen medical symptoms that have persisted over the course of my life and was astonished to find that all my symptoms linked back to the same emotional root causes. The book covers nearly 700 medical conditions including birthing traumas, physical conditions, emotional conditions, addictions, and more. If you're dealing with a longstanding health issue or various medical symptoms that don't seem to want to resolve, I highly recommend using this reference book to direct you to potential emotional root causes.

A few of the most common physical ailments I see in clients include:

» Neck / Shoulder pain: Often a sign of feeling like you're under too much pressure. The pressure may be from an outside source such as work or family responsibilities, or it may be self-inflicted via thought patterns such as perfectionism. Doctors, caregivers, and other health practitioners in stressful situations as well as teachers and individuals in management positions often experience this type of pain.

» Lower back pain: This can be related to the emotion of powerlessness and issues with money, as most people with financial worries feel powerless. This type of pain may also show up in individuals who feel they need to exercise a high level of control over the situations and people in their life.

» Headaches: Associated with fears, headaches can often be triggered by the subconscious as an escape mechanism to get out of a situation.

» Stomach & Digestive Issues / IBS: These issues often stem from constant states of tension (feeling like you need to be extremely cautious in what you say or do, or as though you are always walking on eggshells). There may also be a link with abuse and holding onto anger.

» Joints: The specific joint causing the pain or problem can provide more insight, however in general the emotional themes associated with joints are anger and resentment, as well as fears of taking action or moving forward. There is also a correlation with feeling stuck and not being able to have what you really want.

Take Action

From plantar warts and pimples to more severe problems such as chronic pain or even cancer, digging into your physical symptoms can enlighten and educate you about what's sitting in your attraction point.

Start by making a list of any current or frequently reoccurring physical ailments. Be as detailed as possible, don't leave anything out. For each item on your list, ask yourself the following questions, designed to help you identify root emotional causes.

1. How does your physical ailment make you feel? Trapped? Stuck? Powerless? Helpless? What is your body trying to mirror back to you? If you often lose your voice do you feel like you aren't being heard? If you can't exercise the way you would like to because of an injury, are you feeling angry or powerless?

2. When did the symptom first present itself in your life? What was going on at that time in your life or slightly prior? What emotions does that situation bring up? It's never a surprise that a chronic pain presents itself within the same time frame as a major life trauma.

3. Does the condition come and go? If so, what emotional state are you in when (or just prior to when) the condition re-appears or worsens?

4. Do you benefit in any way from the condition? How does this condition serve you? What does it prevent you from doing or in what way does it help you escape? At

a subconscious level, are you unknowingly creating this condition to aid you in some way? This is known as secondary gain.

5. Make reference to *Metaphysical Anatomy* by Evette Rose (EvetteRose.com). To my knowledge this is the most extensive and detailed reference book linking illness to root emotional causes. It has over 800 pages and includes nearly 700 medical conditions. I use this book with every one of my clients.

#SHIFTCLUB	Ready to take action and get shifting? Log in to Shift Club and download the worksheet titled ***What's My Body Telling Me?*** *http://discoverthepowerofjoy.com/shiftclub*

Understanding Secondary Gain

When it comes to chronic conditions, we may subconsciously feel that we're better off having the condition than we would be if we let it go. As I mentioned above, this is known as "secondary gain." Lets say you work in manual labour and your job is tough, averaging fifty hours a week in a strenuous work environment. One day, while at work, you injure your back. You're now stuck at home, bedridden. Thanks to workers' compensation, you still collect a full salary. Your spouse, also working from home, waits on you hand and foot. You get to stay in bed and watch movies all day. At a certain level, your injury is serving you. You're happier at home, being waited on. If you had a choice, would you choose to remain in this situation or would you rather go back to work? The secondary gain of staying at home may be enough for you to subconsciously tell your body to slow down the healing process, or maybe even prevent it.

A GUIDE TO CLEANING OUT
YOUR INNER INBOX

How much do you care about your teeth? Do you care about them enough to brush them at least once a day? Twice? What about other aspects of your physical body? Do you wash your hair, clean your ears, and trim your nails? How much time do you spend exercising and staying in shape?

Most people care about their physical state of being and their hygiene. Everyone wants to look good and to live a long and healthy life. We all understand the importance of taking care of our physical body because it's the only one we have. When we don't care of it, it begins to break down. Left unbrushed, our teeth would turn yellow and rot. If we didn't exercise, we would gain weight and develop unpleasant health conditions.

It's the same with our inner state of being. When we ignore our emotional health, there are consequences. Others can't see it in the way they might notice physical decay, because most people hide the way they feel or mask feelings such as worry and sadness with medication. Just because others aren't aware of our situation doesn't make it any less important.

What kind of state would your mouth be in if you had never owned a toothbrush or brushed your teeth? Although this analogy isn't pleasant to picture, it represents an accurate depiction of the current inner state of many individuals. We live our entire lives collecting emotional baggage from an early age, and very little is done to clean it up.

Now that I've shared tools to help you identify the emotions and beliefs you may be carrying, the next obvious step is to begin the process of letting them go.

Once released, an emotion you've been storing will no longer impact your attraction point. Your frequency will shift to a new "channel" and you'll begin to attract a different reality. This doesn't mean you will never experience these unwanted emotions again, however the likelihood of circumstances triggering this emotion will diminish. If you believe you've cleared this emotion but it still surfaces on a regular basis, there is a good chance it hasn't fully cleared.

Clearing emotions is a bit of an art form; there is no black and white technique for doing emotional work. Different tools and approaches work differently for different people. For instance, you can clear emotions through yoga or through journaling. One approach may work amazingly well for one person but do very little for another. Over the last decade I've been formally trained in over a dozen different techniques.

When it comes to healing aspects of your physical, mental, or emotional self, there is no one-stop solution to healing. Much of society seeks out the perfect pill with the hopes that it might instantly make their symptoms go away. But, pills often only cover up the symptoms, and don't deal with the root cause, which by now, you know, are your emotional triggers.

Eventually, I realized that since everything is energy, the root cause of ailments must be at an energetic level. And yes, medical and alternative modalities may help to release stuck energy on some levels, but by going straight for the emotions by doing the emotional work, you're targeting the culprits directly responsible for the unwanted energies. In my experience, this allows for more impactful and permanent healing to take place.

The following techniques are some of the go-to techniques that I use with my clients. These techniques directly target the emotions, resulting in a very high success rate. Very rarely have I seen clients not experience results from at least one of the following methods of clearing.

Emotional Freedom Technique (EFT)

Also called "tapping," EFT has been around for approximately two decades and has skyrocketed in popularity over the last few years. EFT is based on the notion that our physical body contains energy meridians. These energy meridians were discovered in Traditional Chinese Medicine and are the basis for the location of acupuncture points. EFT teaches that when we repress emotions, we store them in these energy meridians. By gently tapping on the endpoints of specific major meridians while using certain key statements you are able to release the emotions you've stored. These endpoints are located on the hands, top of the head, around the eyes, nose, chin, collarbone, and under the arm. During a session with an EFT practitioner they will tap on their own body in a specific sequence using specific key statements, and you, as the client, follow along with the practitioner on your own body repeating these statements.

The analogy I use to explain EFT is that of a clogged pipe. Tapping on the meridian endpoints while using statements to target the emotions is similar to shaking or tapping on the pipe. When done right, the effect of tapping will release the emotions from the meridian just as the blockage would release from the pipe. When the release occurs you may feel a slight surge of emotions. Some people may cry, laugh, giggle or yawn. People who are afraid to release emotions using EFT are almost always surprised at how minimally they felt the release and how much lighter they feel after a tapping session.

The reason EFT is my favourite tool is because the focus is on releasing emotions in the most natural way possible, by allowing you to fully feel them. My belief is that it doesn't really matter how the emotions are being stored. What does matter is that this technique is extremely effective at allowing us to feel the emotions we've collected so they can be released. EFT is an extremely simple process. You identify the emotion you want to clear (you don't even need to label it, you can go with "that unpleasant feeling in my stomach") and tap it out. It can be used on emotions, pains, and fears. It can be extremely effective in aiding individuals suffering from anxiety.

Another benefit of EFT is that it uses a rating system called the SUDS scale (standing for Subjective Units of Distress Scale). This scale is used to rank the intensity of the emotion from 0 (non existent) to 10 (as intense as it could ever get). The goal when tapping is to reduce the emotion to 0 where it can no longer be felt. You always start a tapping session by rating an emotion on this scale, then working at it until you hopefully get it down to a 0.

Due to the simplicity of EFT, it is possible to learn how to tap on your own, utilizing books or online instruction videos.

It should be noted that doing EFT without proper training is only marginally effective compared to working with a trained practitioner. An EFT practitioner will lead the session, know to look for specific visual cues, and identify aspects that surface which you may not notice on your own. These aspects need to be cleared to fully release an emotion. Although you can have success learning EFT on your own, I suggest you begin by working with a certified practitioner.

If you just realized for the first time in your life that you should brush your teeth, and picked up a toothbrush, how easy would it be to get your teeth completely clean, to brush away thirty, forty, maybe fifty years of food and plaque? My suggestion would be to book some initial appointments with a dentist. Get your teeth fully and professionally cleaned which will then allow you to then easily maintain your oral hygiene through daily brushing and flossing.

The same goes with clearing the emotions that reside in your inner being. Start by working with a practitioner, someone trained to help you let go of the deeper, more longstanding emotions so that you can then more easily maintain your emotional state and deal with any emotions that may surface in newer circumstances. Using EFT to clear emotions as they come up is much easier than digging into the older emotions at the bottom of your baggage.

EFT is also a great tool to help prevent the collection of any new negative emotions. If I ever feel frustrated by being cut off in traffic, for example, I'll use EFT to tap on whatever negative emotion is present in that moment to ensure it doesn't stick around in my attraction point. EFT is not just a tool you use for a few months to clear a backlog of emotions. I use it to maintain a healthy emotional state and tap a number of times over the course of a week. It's a powerful tool that has become part of my daily life.

If you're interesting in learning EFT and using EFT to clear emotions from your attraction point you can find more information by logging in to Shift Club at *http://discoverthepowerofjoy.com/shiftclub*.

Time Line Therapy

Another technique I find very effective is Time Line Therapy. A Time Line Therapy session can only be done with a trained practitioner. The practitioner guides you through a series of visualizations while in a relaxed state. These visualizations involve floating up above a time line and into the past to a point designated by the subconscious mind where a root emotion may have been experienced. Once arriving at the desired point along the time line, the practitioner can then instruct you to simply let go of the emotion and allow it to float away. Even though this method sounds almost too simplistic, it is extremely effective and often used with individuals wanting to recover from PTSD. I always enjoy doing time line therapy, as clients seem utterly puzzled that an emotion somehow magically disappeared with such little effort.

Meditation

Practices such as yoga and meditation can also be effective to release emotions. I've recorded a popular ten-minute guided meditation called *"The Emotional Freedom Meditation"* (available in Shift Club) that uses a simple visualization based on time line therapy to help you allow negative emotions and pain to float away. Many people who have used it tell me how they've successfully cleared chronic pain or emotion they were unable to release on their own.

Personal Peace Procedure

Imagine yourself, at the moment of birth, being given a beautiful garden filled with rich soil in which you plant your desires. As you experience life, your desires begin to grow. They grow rapidly at first, but as you experience the variety that life has to offer, weeds also begin to take hold. The weeds represent negative emotions and beliefs you've been collecting and broadcasting in your attraction point. Some weeds grow larger than others. These larger weeds are your dominant negative emotions. They have been around much longer and are deeply rooted in your soil.

When you weed your garden, you work on the bigger weeds first - rightfully so. Pulling larger weeds takes a bit more effort and strength; but when completed, gives the most benefit. The same goes with clearing dominant negative emotions as they have the biggest impact on your attraction point. The smaller weeds shouldn't be ignored. Over time they grow larger. Regardless of their size, they are robbing your produce of the life-giving nutrients in the soil. Would you rather those nutrients go to positive aspects you truly want to manifest in your life or the undesirable circumstances?

The personal peace procedure originates from the world of EFT and is designed to help you make peace with experiences of the past. It will assist you in finding every weed growing in your garden, and give you the opportunity to pull each one out.

In EFT we rank emotional charge on a 0 to 10 scale, 0 indicates that the charge is no longer present, while 10 is the most intense sensation of an emotion. This same scale is used when doing a personal peace procedure.

For the personal peace procedure, find a comfortable and quiet space where you can relax. You'll need a pen and paper (or preferably a journal) and enough time so that you don't feel rushed.

Start by recollecting your earliest memory. Go all the way back to the day you were born. Pull up the data bank of experiences from your memory and go through them in chronological order. For every memory with a negative emotional charge, write it down. It could be that time you were scolded by your parents or a teacher, locked in the closet by a sibling, picked on by someone on the school bus, or left behind at a party in college. Don't leave any experience out, as each memory that holds a negative charge is a weed growing in the garden of your attraction point. Take your time. This may take twenty minutes or two hours, the length of time does not matter. You can always go back and repeat the exercise at a later date.

Once you've identified all the negatively charged memories, go through the list and rank their emotional charge on the 0 to 10 scale. This will help you identify which weeds are biggest and which emotional charges you'll want to clear first.

When doing emotional work, the following should be taken into consideration regardless of what tool is being used. These factors are the most important when it comes to working on releasing negative emotions:

1. Working with a trained practitioner is the quickest and most effective way to clear unwanted emotions. There are several do-it-yourself tools you can use on your own, but nothing compares to working with a practitioner. If your car was having engine problems, you would be

much better off taking it to a trained mechanic than trying to investigate and resolve the problem yourself. A mechanic is trained to identify the core issue with your engine and knows exactly what is creating that ticking sound and where to look. The same goes with emotional clearing work. If you work with a good practitioner they should be trained to know what to look for and where to guide you to get the best possible results. Working with them usually requires a financial investment but the benefit of letting go of negative emotions is invaluable. Releasing these negative emotions will have a priceless impact on all aspects of your life.

2. When selecting a method for clearing, choose a technique that feels good to you. It may take a few sessions to gain confidence using a specific technique, but if it doesn't feel like it's getting results, try something different. You may need to try a few different things before you learn what works best. The same goes with selecting a practitioner. Regardless of the technique being used, it is critical to work with someone with whom you feel safe and whom you trust.

3. Be patient and go easy on yourself. You'll be clearing emotions that have been around for years, if not decades. This doesn't mean they will take a long time to clear, however, don't expect to be completely clear overnight. Most of my clients see major shifts within about three to five sessions. Everyone processes emotions differently. Some individuals can clear major emotions in one or two sessions while for others it may take five, six or even more.

4. There is nothing to fear. Emotions can't hurt you; they are simply energies sitting in your energy meridians (more on this in a bit). You may be afraid of emotional work because of the feelings that surface, but knowing these emotions could be negatively impacting your well-being, and the circumstances in your life, wouldn't it be best to allow yourself to feel the emotions for a few seconds and then let them go, perhaps forever?

5. It isn't necessary to recollect painful memories to release the emotions relevant to past experiences. With techniques such as time line therapy that help release emotions through the subconscious mind, you don't have to worry about recalling unpleasant past events. (More on time line therapy in the next section.)

6. Clearing emotions is easier than you think. With the right practitioner, the process can be quick, easy, and extremely effective. No emotion is impossible to clear as long as you are ready and willing to let the emotion go.

The next step? Use the technique that feels best to you and get clearing. If you're serious about releasing your baggage, get in touch with a practitioner and start working with them. If working with a practitioner is out of your budget or you're inclined to work on clearing emotions on your own, you can get access to EFT follow-along tapping videos as well as the Emotional Freedom Meditation in Shift Club. Keep in mind, however, that working with a trained practitioner is often the best and fastest way to clear emotions.

How do you know if you're doing it right? If you're successful at clearing the emotions - pulling out the weeds - you will begin to notice you feel lighter, like a weight has been lifted off your shoulders. The things that used to trigger you emotionally will lessen or completely disappear. You may notice that clearing the emotional charge around one event reduces or clears the emotional charge present with other events.

When clearing emotions you may unexpectedly get phone calls from friends or loved ones. You may find they are starting to act differently, in more positive ways. This is direct reflection of the changes that are occurring in your attraction point.

Once your personal peace procedure is complete and you've cleared the charge from all the events on your list, you'll notice that these memories no longer bring up negative emotions. Events, which when previously recollected would have angered or saddened you, may now simply be memories with no emotional attachment.

Take Action

When working with negative emotions, remember that the emotions you carry are not part of you. You picked these emotions up along your journey and you can also let them go. The amount of time it takes to let go of emotions is dependent on multiple factors and will be different for everyone. I've had clients let go of lifelong emotions such as rejection and unworthiness in just one session while for others it has taken significantly more work.

When choosing a strategy for letting go of your emotions, I encourage you to work with a well-trained practitioner to aid in the process. Working with someone who knows exactly how to find and clear your repressed emotions will assist you in letting them go more rapidly and with greater ease. Attempting to clear negative emotions on your own could take months. Working with a practitioner will cut this time down drastically. Dominant negative emotions are often the most difficult to clear, yet will have the most significant positive impact when released. I suggest, at a minimum, working with a practitioner to release your dominant negative emotions.

When choosing a practitioner, work with someone with whom you feel comfortable and safe, and who is trained in tools specific to clearing emotions. I suggest working with someone trained in EFT. After a few sessions with an EFT practitioner you'll have cleared some of your emotional baggage, and will likely know enough to use tapping on your own. I use tapping as a primary tool with all my clients and always have great success. It's easy, effective, and very powerful.

Ready to take action and get shifting? Log in to Shift Club and start clearing unwanted emotions. You may want to try the **Emotional Freedom Meditation**, watch some of the EFT tapping videos, or book a session with a practitioner. *http://discoverthepowerofjoy.com/shiftclub*

Clearing – Final Notes

You want to ensure that the emotions you're working on are fully cleared so that they no longer impact your attraction point. When you've fully cleared an emotion, you should feel lighter. The emotion should not surface as frequently, and you should no longer attract situations that repeatedly bring up this emotion. A few final notes to contribute to your success:

1. **Commit to yourself.** Commit to this process. Clearing negative emotions will have a long-term, positive

impact on your health, your well-being, and on the circumstances you draw in your life. If you've identified negative emotions, don't ignore them or play them down.

2. **Identify.** Start by identifying your dominant negative emotions. Clearing them first will create the biggest positive impact. They may be more deeply rooted but this does not signify that they will be more difficult to clear. Identify these emotions by looking into what negative emotions currently surface for you the most. Second, look at past experiences. See if you can identify a pattern in the emotions that frequently surface. Use the probing question: "How does this situation or circumstance make me feel?"

3. **Clear.** Once you've identified your dominant negative emotions, get clearing. Use a process that feels good and take advantage of the tools available in Shift Club (*http://discoverthepowerofjoy.com/shiftclub*). Don't be afraid to reach out and work with a practitioner.

4. **Take notice.** Once dominant negative emotions begin to clear you should notice a difference almost right away. You'll likely feel lighter and things that might have bothered you in the past may no longer trigger you. You may feel healthier and notice certain aches and pains have diminished or even completely disappeared. Over a longer period of time you may notice the people and situation around you begin to change. You may start to notice problems beginning to resolve themselves or solutions beginning to show up effortlessly.

5. **Keep going.** Once you feel like you've made a significant dent in, or fully cleared out your dominant negative emotions, don't stop there. Shift your focus to the personal peace procedure. You've cleared out the larger weeds in your garden and now you're ready for the smaller ones. You may want to run this exercise multiple times, maybe even a few times a year. Ensure that anything that creeps in gets noticed right away so you can clear emotions you may have unwittingly decided to hang on to.

6. **Maintain.** You've worked hard to clear the emotions that hold you back. Keep your garden clean. As you continue to work through and release the negative emotions you've collected from your past, don't forget to maintain your garden. When negative emotions surface, clear them immediately rather than hanging on to them by covering them up or attempting to push them aside. Dedicate time on a weekly or monthly basis to check in on how you feel and clear any emotions you may have picked up.

When it comes to your health and well-being you've likely spent most of your life focused on physical health from an outer world perspective. The build-up of unwanted emotions in your inner inbox is inevitable and you will want to work with your emotions to clean it up. Maintaining the health of our inner state of being is not readily discussed in our society. In fact, there is still a stigma around seeking help with emotional work, believing this type of work should be reserved for those suffering from major anxiety, depression, or mental illness. Nothing could be further from the truth. Everyone experiences some form of trauma in his or her life. Everyone has latched on to and is carrying negative emotions. Seeing someone who can assist you in releasing these emotions is one of the most life-changing decisions you can make.

Seeking assistance isn't just about shifting away from a state of sadness. Many of my clients are happy, successful people who require assistance with specific aspects of their life, such as relationships or weight. These people have spent their whole lives harbouring feelings such as rejection, powerlessness, and lack of self-worth, just under the surface. While these emotions have not caused a clinical diagnosis such as depression, they have certainly impacted aspects of these clients' lives, such as the ability to maintain healthy relationships or the ability to move away from unwanted circumstances.

Sara recently came to me because she no longer knew where to turn. Divorced once already, she felt that for her, being in a loving, peaceful relationship was next to impossible. Due to early childhood experiences, she had grown up with deep feelings of rejection and low self-worth. Like a volcano on the verge of eruption, her longstanding feelings of rejection were always on the surface ready to explode. The slightest circumstance would trigger irrational fights between Sara and her various partners. It would come to the point where the man in her life would no longer be able to work overtime or have a night out with his buddies without significant emotional reaction on her part. Sara recognized her behavior was irrational, unhealthy, and unfair, but was unable to tame it. This debilitating behavior was responsible for the demise of her marriage and continued to impact all of her relationships.

When Sara and I met for the first time, she expressed the thought that this behavior would be impossible to clear. She had felt rejected for so long that she believed the emotion was part of her. She didn't remember what it felt like *not* to feel this feeling of rejection. It was all she ever consciously knew. I reassured her that at birth, she was born in a perfect state of being, but had acquired the feelings of rejection over time. Just like with a software system, it was simply a matter of identifying and reprogramming the root cause, and removing the unwanted program, which was the emotion of rejection, coupled with negative beliefs around self-worth.

After two sessions in the span of five days, Sara completely released these negative emotions. Her behaviour in relationships completely shifted, as did the type of men she attracted. No longer did she attract men who brought out her feelings of low self-worth, rather she was freed to attract relationships with men that both nurtured and empowered her.

Notice what emotions you are harbouring and the negative consequences these aspects may have on your reality. Up to now, has your health focus been exclusively on outer world aspects such as nutrition, exercise, and brushing your teeth? Now that you recognize the importance of maintaining the health of your inner being, are you ready to take the next step towards an even healthier life? If you knew that your inner being was filled with cavities would you continue to ignore it? These aspects, until cleared, will continue to negatively impact both the state of your well-being, and your outer world experiences. However, as Sara experienced, the process of clearing out the unwanted aspects of your inner being can be relatively quick and easy and produce life-changing results.

HOW TO CREATE LIFE CHANGING MOMENTUM

GROWING UP IN CANADA, I spent many a winter's day zipping down snow-covered ski slopes. If you've skied much at all, you know that, like driving a car or riding a bike, the direction in which you will go down the hill is directly related to where your gaze is focused. If you're continually focused toward the left side of a fork in the trail, where all the moguls, trees, and rough patches are, that is exactly where you will most likely end up, bumping and lurching all along the way. However, if you put your focus on the right side of the fork in the trail, the nicely groomed, beautifully smooth trail, you'll have a much easier and more pleasant ride. The more time you spend focused in the direction you don't want to go, the higher the chances are that you'll end up there.

The same is the true for your thoughts. The attention you give to a subject is an invitation to bring more of that subject into your reality.

Take a second now and reflect on the first few things that went through your mind this morning. Did you focus on the unpleasant things that could potentially surface today or the things you were really looking forward to? The bills, deadlines, and morning traffic, or the beauty of the sunrise, appreciation for phone chat you had last night, and the time you get to spend with your friends at lunch today?

When you wake up, your mind is in a neutral state. It has no momentum. This is potentially the most critical moment of your day. It's the moment you get to choose what direction you want your thoughts to take and impacts how your entire day will play out.

Choice number one: focus on the negative: The upcoming meeting you don't feel prepared for. Your boss getting on your case like he does every other day. The traffic delays due to construction on the highway. This will throw your thoughts into a negative spiral. When a snowball begins to roll down the side of a mountain it gets bigger and bigger, gradually increasing in both size and velocity. The bigger it gets, the faster it travels, and the harder it will be to stop. Your thoughts, as you go about your day, also build momentum. When a thought enters your mind, a second thought soon follows. And a third, a fourth, and a fifth. If the first thought is negative, odds are, the thoughts that follow will be negative as well.

The second (and optimal) choice is to focus on creating positive momentum as soon as you wake up. Setting this intent will create an avalanche of positive thoughts which in turn will attract positive experiences. The effects may seem subtle and take a bit of effort initially but over time the results will become apparent. I've had clients and workshop attendees report back to me that the mere act of doing gratitude journaling each morning when waking up had a significantly positive impact on their lives after only three weeks.

Positive Daily Practice

One of the first things I do with every new client is to help him or her set up a positive daily practice. The goal of this practice is to train yourself to create positive momentum as early as possible in your day, before negative thoughts or momentum have any opportunity to creep in. Once your positive momentum has reached a high point, your goal is then to hold this good feeling place as long as you can throughout the day.

At first, like a gym routine, it may feel like effort, but as you learn to build more positive momentum, the process will get easier. Incorporating a 30-minute practice into every morning might initially seem to take away time from another part of your day. However, this practice will help you achieve that state of flow where your productivity will increase to the point where you'll actually get more done in less time and with less effort. In the beginning you may find you can only hold this good feeling for a few hours (or perhaps even just a few minutes on those tricky days) but with a bit of consistency and dedication, the benefit of the positive practice will soon become apparent.

What does a positive daily practice look like? Remember that the goal is to feel good and everyone's practice will be a little different. What I suggest is to start with some gratitude journaling as soon as you wake up, even before getting out of bed, if possible. Making a gratitude list in your head will do but writing it down is always preferable. Shifting the momentum of your thoughts towards the positive should always be the top priority. I also suggest ending your practice with a quick 15-minute meditation, followed by a visualization of your entire day. Watch your entire day play out on a screen in your mind as perfectly as you could imagine. I like to visualize my sessions with each of my clients, seeing them leave the session happy, having experienced exciting shifts in the way they feel and the way they respond to the world around them. I see myself getting all the best parking spots, spending quality time with my family and friends, and having amazing meals. I visualize myself fully enjoying my day right up until my head hits the pillow at the end of the day.

Between the gratitude journal and meditation, add any activities that pump you up and make you feel good. Sing and dance to music you love. Get some exercise and spend time in nature. I like to go for a walk on the beach, hop on the elliptical trainer, and eat healthy foods that make my cells happy. Feel free to mix it up. Your goal isn't a routine for the sake of having a routine, your goal is to feel good. Like any new diet or gym routine, begin at your own pace. It might be easier to start with one thing and then add in some others. Have fun with it and don't let it stress you out.

Another beneficial exercise, coming from the teachings of Abraham-Hicks, is to write lists of positive aspects. Every morning during your practice, write three to five pages of positive aspects around a situation in life where you're looking for improvement. If you were a musician looking to win an audition or master a specific technique, I would suggest writing a few pages on the positive aspects around your playing. Those aspects you appreciate. If you're looking for more money, write about the aspects around money that make you feel good. If you're looking to love yourself more or improve on a physical condition or lose weight, write about the aspects of your body that currently feel good and cultivate appreciation for them. This positive aspects exercise is extremely powerful and helps create positive momentum by focusing on those things that feel good to you.

Take Action

Aside from clearing work, creating positive momentum is the most important thing you can do to create a significant shift. Your goal is to feel as good as you possibly can, early in the day, and to hold this feeling for as long as you possibly can.

Spend some time coming up with an action plan for you daily practice. Do you need to get up thirty minutes earlier? What will your positive daily practice look like? Are you able to wake up just 20 minutes earlier so that you can write in your gratitude journal, meditate and visualize your perfect day? What else can you squeeze in between your gratitude work and journaling so that you can create positive momentum for your day? Commit to applying your practice one day at a time. Over time your practice will flow with greater ease and eventually, like brushing your teeth, you won't want to go a single day without it.

 #SHIFTCLUB

Ready to take action and get shifting? Log in to Shift Club and download the worksheet titled **_The Morning Practice Roadmap_**. _http://discoverthepower-ofjoy.com/shiftclub_

Take Note.

At the end of your day spend some time reflecting on how your positive momentum played out. Were you able to hold it for a few minutes, a few hours, or the entire day? At what point did you allow your momentum to shift and what circumstances did you allow to shift it? If the same circumstances present themselves tomorrow, how can you shift your point of focus so that you don't allow your positive momentum to be impacted by those circumstances? What emotion or thoughts do you believe may be sitting in your attraction point that may have attracted those unwanted circumstances? Don't judge yourself if you have a bad day, some days will be easier than others. Give yourself a high five for making the effort and remember that the more you stick with it, the further along you'll get.

POWERFUL PROCESSES

ALONG WITH THE AMAZING tools and techniques you've been shown so far, I'm going to share with you some of the top processes I use for myself and also assign to my clients. These powerful processes originate from varying sources and have been around for a number of years. In Shift Club (*http://discoverthepowerofjoy.com/shiftclub*), you'll find examples of each of these processes as well as worksheets to help you apply them.

Automatic Writing

Automatic writing is a journaling technique to help tune into your emotions, and help release them. It's a natural reaction for us to want to ignore negative emotions and turn our back to them. Often we don't realize those emotions are present, even though we do know a situation or past circumstance feels heavy.

Sometimes facing negative emotions and acknowledging them is all that is needed to let them go. Through the automatic writing process we can allow this to happen more easily by dis-engaging the conscious mind and writing without thought.

Depending on the person, automatic writing may feel diffi-cult or clunky at first, or, alternatively, may feel totally natural. The key to properly applying automatic writing is to try and keep a continuous flow without reflecting upon what's being put on paper until after you've completed the exercise.

Start by choosing a situation where you feel negative emo-tion or heavy feelings. It could be a past event or a current cir-cumstance in your life. As you put your focus on this situation, simply allow the pen to glide over the page, and write, write, write. Don't even think about what you're writing, don't judge, or edit the content, just let the words flow. Some of what flows out from the end of your pen may not even make any sense at all.

If at any point in the exercise you feel stuck, try asking some of the probing questions. How does that situation make me feel? How does his response make me feel? In what way did that feel unsafe? What is the worse thing about that? Keep writing, you may end up with half a page or you may fill out four or five pages.

As the words flow, emotion may begin to surface. Allow yourself to fully feel these emotions, their appearance is a sign that they are present and looking to be released. Crying, yawn-ing, and laughing are all positive signs indicating emotional release. Remember, emotions aren't able to harm you and by allowing yourself to feel them and let them go, you will feel lighter and closer to your natural state of joy.

Once you've completed the process you can review the results of your automatic writing session a few times. You may be surprised at some of the things that came up and gain new awareness or understanding of thoughts or beliefs you may not have been aware were present.

When to use automatic writing?

When you're having a hard time letting go of a specific situation or circumstance or when you're having difficulty releasing negative emotions. Any time a circumstance in your life feels heavy, uncomfortable or stuck, you can apply this exercise to try and flush out negative emotions around it and get at the root cause.

#SHIFTCLUB

Ready to take action and get shifting? Log in to Shift Club and download the worksheet titled ***The Automatic Writing Worksheet***. *http://discoverthepower-ofjoy.com/shiftclub*

Focus Wheel

The focus wheel is another process originating from Abraham-Hicks. The purpose of a focus wheel is to help you alter a belief and shift the way you feel in relation to a specific circumstance. This exercise is called a focus wheel because it involves creating a wheel with 12 spokes. The best way to visualize the wheel is by imagining a 12-slice pie with a circle smack dab in the center.

1. Start by identifying what it is you don't want. If you just ended a relationship for example your "don't want" might be to attract another partner who doesn't love or appreciate you the way you want to be appreciated.

2. Next, identify - based on what you don't want - what it is that you really do want. Write this desire down in the center of your wheel. In this example, your desire

might be to attract a relationship where you feel loved and appreciated.

3. Beginning at the twelve o'clock position in your wheel, write down, in this pie slice, the best-feeling statement you can find that re-affirms the desire you wrote down.

4. Continue filling in each pie slice with a re-affirming statement, building more and more momentum as you go until you've gone all the way around the circle. You should begin to feel your energy rise with each new statement.

5. Once you've gone all the way around the circle, you can end here or continue writing more statements if they continue to flow.

In our example, where your desire is to attract a relationship that makes you feel loved and appreciated, your focus wheel might be made up of statements like the following:

»   I have experienced loved and appreciation in the past.

»   I imagine I can probably experience love and appreciation again in the future.

»   I know of others who definitely feel loved and appreciated in their current relationships.

»   I eventually always get what is best for me, and I know that by tapping and clearing negative emotions around this relationship I'll be one step closer to this desire.

»   I feel like that person might be just around the corner.

»   Every day I learn to love and appreciate myself more, and know this will help me manifest the ideal partner into my reality.

The focus wheel process can feel challenging at first, but the more you do it the easier it will get. Once mastered, the process is extremely powerful in shifting the way you feel and is a powerful tool for aligning your belief with the vibration of your desires.

When to use a focus wheel?

You can do a few focus wheels daily! It's a great exercise for your morning practice or any time you recognize a limiting belief or doubt creeping in around a desire.

Ready to take action and get shifting? Log in to Shift Club and download the worksheet titled **Focus Wheel**. *http://discoverthepowerofjoy.com/shiftclub*

Sacred Container

The sacred container isn't what you might typically think of as a container in the physical sense. Rather it is metaphysical container, in the form of a hand-written intention, used to help you get clear on a desire so that your inner being knows exactly what you want. Vision boards are a popular form of general intention setting, however, it's always better to get as specific as possible. When working with clients we always define specific goals and I have them create a sacred container representing the manifested state of these goals. In other words, write the story as if it has already happened.

The biggest mistake you can make when creating a sacred container is not getting specific enough. A big misconception is that the more general you are, the easier it will be to manifest. Not only is this false, it will often result in a slightly different manifestation than you anticipated, as was the case in my owl story. But don't put too much emphasis on physical details. Most people focus too much on the physical details of their desire rather than the feelings that go along with them. When you write the story, don't only describe the appearance of the manifestation. Record how it makes you feel. What emotions does having this manifestation bring to you? What sounds do you hear? How does it feel when you touch it? Use all your senses and get as descriptive as possible. Have fun with it.

The following excerpt is part of a sacred container Anik used to manifest her dream job in a local health food store:

> "Things flow so easily and effortlessly when working at the store. I feel comfortable with the work I do. My salary supplies all my needs and more. I get so many amazing perks, deals, and gifts. I enjoy organizing the products in the store and we all work so well together. Communication flows easily between all staff members. I enjoy learning and discovering about all of our products. I feel as though I am very well organized. I get so much done with very little effort. The store has a positive, powerful, and attractive reputation. Many people and customers are attracted to us. This store is my store, my haven, my playground."

When to use a sacred container?

You can create a sacred container any time a new desire pops into your head. Once completed, you can set it aside. If your desire changes, you add to it, or write a new one but remember, using *feeling* words is key!

#SHIFTCLUB	Ready to take action and get shifting? Log in to Shift Club and download the worksheet titled **The Desire Realization Worksheet**. *http://discoverthepower-ofjoy.com/shiftclub*

Positive Aspect Lists

Creating a list of positive aspects is another process recommended by Abraham-Hicks. Of all the process I've outlined in this book, the creation of lists of positive aspects is definitely my favourite. Abraham-Hicks recommends having a journal (called your Book of Positive Aspects) dedicated solely to creating lists of things you love about certain topics, and this is one exercise I never skip when doing my morning practice.

Set a timer and dedicate a specific amount of time to writing down lists of positive aspects centering on various topics. Choose a topic such as money and write down aspects around money in your experience that make you feel good. As you write each aspect down, consciously allow yourself to feel the pleasant emotions in regard to this subject. Positive aspects around money could include entries such as "I made enough money to pay all my bills this month and travel to visit my sister" or "Sales felt easier than ever this month, and that bonus feels closer than ever."

During my morning practice I usually choose three topics and spend five to ten minutes on each one. You can write about situations in your life that are going well or situations that aren't going well, for which you want to shift the momentum. Common topics include money, relationships, career, and health.

When to do a list of positive aspects?

I highly suggest doing a list of positive aspects daily during your morning practice, right after appreciation journaling since the two exercises are somewhat similar and build upon one another. However, you can do a list of positive aspects anytime throughout the day. The positive aspects list can help shift your momentum if you feel as though you need a quick pick-me-up or a positive shift in the way you feel.

<table>
<tr><td>#SHIFTCLUB</td><td>Ready to take action and get shifting? Log in to Shift Club and download the worksheet titled **The Positive Aspects Worksheet**. *http://discoverthepowerofjoy. com/shiftclub*</td></tr>
</table>

Polarity Processing

Polarity processing was taught to me by one of my coaches. The analogy I like to use is that of an old cartoon where a character such as Bugs Bunny is faced with a dilemma. On one shoulder sits a character, dressed like an angel. On the other shoulder, that same character, dressed as the devil. The angel and the devil have conflicting views on what decision the character should make, and this represents the two polarities.

Often times, at a subconscious level, we stop ourselves from being able to move forward in a situation or we stall on taking action. This happens when two opposing parts of our mind are in disagreement in terms of how to proceed. Part of us believes that one direction is the best course of action while another part of us thinks just the opposite. Since our mind is at a stalemate, we end up stalling and not going anywhere.

Can you think of a situation in your life where part of you wants one thing but another part of you wants something else? Remaining in a relationship versus ending a relationship? Buying a new house versus staying put? Having another child versus leaving things the way they are? If you feel as though you're stuck in a situation where there are two polarities, then doing a polarity processing exercise can be extremely beneficial.

The goal of polarity processing isn't to come up with a list of pros and cons that will help you make a final decision. The goal is to look at every aspect of each polarity, both the positive and the negative, so that you can flush out all your beliefs. As in automatic writing, you'll want to write stream of consciousness style, so that you're keeping your conscious mind as disengaged as possible. Once completed you can then re-read what you've written and possibly gain new awareness.

Start by identifying the two polarities. As an example, let's pretend you're debating whether you want to stay in a relationship or leave it. In this case you'll have the following two polarities:

Polarity 1: Stay in the relationship.
Polarity 2: Leave the relationship.

For each polarity you're then going to want to explore two aspects, the desire and the fear.

Take a blank sheet of paper and divide it into four quadrants as if you were drawing a giant "plus" sign, radiating from the center of the paper. Next you're going to label each of the four quadrants. The top two should be dedicated to the first polarity and the bottom two for the second polarity:

Top half of the page:

Quadrant 1: Desire to <polarity 1> (Desire to stay in the relationship)
Quadrant 2: Fear of <polarity 1> (Fear of staying in the relationship)

Bottom half of the page:

Quadrant 3: Desire to <polarity 2> (Desire to leave the relationship)
Quadrant 4: Fear of <polarity 2> (Fear of leaving the relationship)

Next, for each quadrant write down all your thoughts and feelings corresponding to each section. Just like in the automatic writing process discussed earlier in this chapter, you'll want to keep writing until there's nothing left to write. If you run out of room, continue on another page. Don't move onto the next quadrant until you're finished with the current quadrant.

By the time you're done, each quadrant will look something like this:

"Desire to stay in the relationship (Quadrant 1): Won't break his heart, won't need to move out, won't be alone again, others won't judge me for leaving, want to remain stable, comfortable here, won't miss the dog, financial ease, easier to stay, may never find someone else who loves me, I want kids sooner than later, …"

Once you've completed the exercise, you can re-read the entries to see if you've gained any new awareness. Even if nothing new has surfaced in the writing you'll often gain a greater sense of inner peace or clarity around the situation, having felt like you've looked at all the angles.

When to use polarity processing?

Polarity process isn't an exercise I use as often as focus wheel or positive aspects. It can be used when you have an important decision to make or feel stuck in a situation and unsure how to proceed. I suggest trying any of the following aspects to see what might come up. These include: success versus failure, wealthy versus poor, powerful versus powerless, and give versus receive.

#SHIFTCLUB	Ready to take action and get shifting? Log in to Shift Club and download the worksheet titled **The Polarity Processing Worksheet**. *http://discoverthepowerofjoy.com/shiftclub*

THE BIG THREE – MANIFESTING
MONEY, RELATIONSHIPS AND PURPOSE

HAVE YOU EVER TRIED to guess the things people want to manifest most when it comes to the law of attraction? Observing law of attraction communities online seems to show money is at the top of the list, with relationships falling in close second and life purpose trailing behind, a distant third. These are what I call the big three. If you're reading this book you're likely after one - or maybe all - of these three things.

Entire books have been written on each one of these topics and for good reason. Not only are these the things people want most, they are also the things that can be the most difficult to manifest. In this chapter you'll learn about each of the big three, why most people are stuck when it comes to manifesting what they want, and the action steps needed to create a shift.

Manifesting Money

One thing almost everyone desires is more money. When working with clients who are looking to shift their financial abundance there is always one common theme. They've tried everything. They may have hired the top sales people to sell their product or have worked with the best marketers. They've tried every tactic in the book to make more money, yet they keep hitting metaphorical brick walls.

So what is it that these clients have been doing wrong?

They have been trying to create a shift through outward action when the shift needs to take place in their attraction point.

I remember an Abraham-Hicks recording where Abraham explained that you can have two individuals who look the same, act the same, and sell the same product with the same branding and marketing. But, even though all the outward factors are identical, one has record sales while the other isn't selling a thing. Why would this be? It's because they both have different beliefs and emotions in their attraction point.

I've seen large sums of money manifest extremely quickly for some of my clients. A mere week after one of my workshops, one participant discovered he was entitled to double the pension amount he had previously been led to believe. Another person manifested the exact amount of money she needed for a family trip within a few days of a clearing session. I've personally manifested a five-figure sum of money just two weeks after deciding to take a month off from working and asking the universe to fill in the gap.

So if it's possible for money to manifest quickly and easily like this, why is so hard for some people to manifest? What are the biggest money blockers?

There are three key elements you should look at when it comes to money blocks:

1. Emotions of powerlessness, lack of control, and feeling stuck: A good sign you're carrying any of these emotions is if you suffer from frequent lower back problems. How does not having any, or even just enough, money make you feel? Remember that you attract experiences reflecting your inner state of being. If you hold onto feelings of being stuck or of powerlessness, your reality will reflect that back to you. You need to work on maintaining feelings of freedom and power if you want to resonate at a level that attracts money.

2. Limiting beliefs picked up from your parents during childhood or during other life circumstances: If there is one aspect of our reality that can hold a lot of limiting beliefs, it's money. Here are just a few statements that might sound familiar: Money doesn't grow on trees. People with money are selfish. You need to work hard for money. Money is the root of evil. Money breaks families apart. People will judge me. I'll lose all my friends. I'm irresponsible with money and would lose it all. If you want to start identifying your money blocks, use the belief-probing question. In what way would having a lot of money make me feel unsafe? I've had multiple clients with money blocks that were related to how their partners spent money. The subconscious self-sabotaging behaviour was pushing them to lose or dwindle their income to almost nothing because it was safer to stop manifesting money than to deal with their partners' unhealthy spending habits.

3. Be aware of your focus point: As you read in my experience with bees, you get more of whatever you focus

upon. Most people are busier noticing all the money going out than they are celebrating its coming in. The end result? There's more money going out! If your focus is on debt and lack of money, rather than on the in-flow of money (no matter how big or how little) that you are experiencing, you'll continue to attract more expenses and more debt. As oxymoronic as it may sound, you are essentially creating an abundance of lack. This is the case for many people, and in the beginning stages at least, it may be prudent to give as little attention as possible to your finances. Pay your bills as best you can and don't put any extra focus on money unless you're feeling good about your money situation and able to appreciate the money that is flowing in your direction.

Other factors come into play as well. For instance, one client who had a seven figure net worth and fell into bankruptcy not once, but twice, realized that his money flow stopped when he decided to stop drinking and partying and to take life more seriously. Although limiting beliefs could have been at play, the result in his financial shift was likely due to resistance induced by closing up his receiving channel by getting too serious about life.

A number of years ago I made a new friend named Denise at a shamanic journeying workshop. The two-day workshop was given by a couple that had flown in from the United States. Of the twenty-six participants, Denise stood out above the rest. Her stories and her connection to spirit were amazing and she was an obvious natural talent when it came to shamanic work. At the end of the workshop, the facilitators approached Denise and invited her to join them in attending a month-long training that would take place later in the year. Although Denise was excited about the opportunity, she didn't have the funds to attend, due to the high price of the course and the extensive travel costs.

Although Denise had accepted the fact she would not be able to attend, the training haunted her. Friends, who were excited for Denise, continually asked if she was going. Newsletters would appear in her inbox reminding her of the event.

Denise grew frustrated. A few weeks prior to the registration deadline she had finally had enough and yelled out to the universe in frustration, "I get it! I can see you want me there but I don't have the money. If you want me to attend, you need to make the money show up!" Over the next few weeks something magical occurred. She unexpectedly received a cheque in the mail from a workers' compensation claim where an accounting error had been noticed and rectified. A few days later, her husband also received unexpected money from a miscalculation in an income tax refund. The total amount of the two cheques? Just under six thousand dollars. One hundred dollars more than she needed to attend the workshop, which she joyfully did.

Why do I believe the money suddenly manifested with so much ease? Because Denise gave in and stopped resisting the fact that she didn't have the money. She fully released the responsibility for making the money show up, handing it over to the universe, thus releasing all pressure-driven resistance of needing to make it happen herself.

Manifesting Money – Action Steps

» Emotional Probing: Ask how not having enough money makes you feel. Work on clearing the negative emotion that surfaces. Use the tapping videos in Shift Club for these specific emotions.

» Belief Probing: If you had millions of dollars manifest tomorrow, what would be the worst thing about having all that money? What's the worst thing that could happen? In what way would having all that money feel unsafe for you? Work on clearing these beliefs.

» Focus Work: Begin to put as little focus as possible on the lack of money while you spend as much time as you can being appreciative of the money coming in. If you win one hundred dollars, leave it in your wallet so you're noticing all the money you have there. Keep noticing all the abundance around you. The abundance of water to drink. The abundance or fresh air. The more abundance you notice the more abundance you'll attract.

» Morning Practice: Spend at least five minutes each morning writing a list of positive aspects around your financial situation and money. You can even do this twice a day if possible. Positive aspects might include money coming in, finding a quarter on the sidewalk, or the fact that you made more money this month than last month. Take any positive aspects you can find around your finances and magnify them!

» Other Exercises: Do a focus wheel on money as well as polarity processing exercises with the polarities of poor versus wealthy, stuck versus free, powerful versus powerless, abundance versus lack.

Ready to take action and get shifting? Log in to Shift Club and download the worksheet titled **The Money Breakthrough Worksheet.** *http://discoverthepowerofjoy.com/shiftclub*

#SHIFTCLUB

Manifesting Relationships

When it comes to manifesting your soul mate or a happi-ly-ever-after relationship, the most important thing you need to realize is that, like money, you're going to attract more of what-ever you are focused on. When it comes to relationships, you're going to attract someone that reflects the way you feel about you. For example, if your inner inbox is filled with emotions of loneliness then you'll likely attract a partner who will reflect this emotion back to you in some way. I often see clients who struggle with powerlessness end up attracting a partner who doesn't listen to them or makes them feel like they are never being heard. I love using relationships in my digging work with clients because they are extremely telling about what they have going on.

Take some time and explore your past relationships and their commonalities. If you're like most people, you'll notice that in one way or another they bring up the same negative emotions. You can also likely trace this negative emotion back to your childhood. If so, you've found a dominant negative emotion and are one step closer to letting it go.

If you're seeking to attract a partner, the number one piece of advice I have for you is to stop looking for someone else to make you happy. When Anik and I met, we had both ended our marriages and were focused on our own inner growth. Nei-ther one of us were looking for someone else to bring us joy or to compliment who we were. We were concerned with our own happiness and inner growth without the need for an exter-nal relationship. We were busy fostering our relationship with ourselves.

The most successful, long-lasting, harmonious, and healthy relationships are those where there is no co-dependency between the two individuals. It's never someone else's responsibility to make you happy and it's never your responsibility to compromise yourself to make someone else happy. The most magical part of the relationship between Anik and I is our mutual self-respect. Not only for the choices we make, but also for the ability each of us has to recognize that our emotional state is our own responsibility and nobody else's. I never put pressure on her or expect her to do things for me and she never puts that pressure on me.

Lack of safety is another important concern in the context of relationships. Many people suffer from self-sabotaging patterns due to a feeling of a lack of safety in relationships. Have you ever suffered from mental, emotional, or physical abuse? Have you ever been cheated on or had your heart broken? Have you ever been controlled in a relationship or had to do things you didn't want to do? Have you ever suffered from a heart-wrenching, unexpected break up?

These are all circumstances that can create fears, at conscious or subconscious levels, which can result in self-sabotaging patterns and relationship blocks. Once again, digging work around emotions and beliefs can help bring up your blocks so they can be fully dealt with and cleared.

Manifesting Relationships – Action Steps

» Focusing on You: If your focus is on relationships, whether improving a current relationship or attracting a new one, your sole focus should be on you. What emotional gaps are you looking to fill through a relationship? In what aspect do you not feel whole as a single person? What void do you believe exists by not having a partner? How much do you love yourself? How do you perceive yourself? These are all important questions you will want to ask yourself so that you can work on being complete without the need of another person. If any of the answers to these questions bring up answers that don't feel very good, it's an indication that these are areas that you could work on.

» Emotional Probing: Spend some time looking at each of your relationships. How do the negative aspects of these relationships make you feel? Do similar emotions and circumstances surface in all these relationships? Do these emotions also correlate to your childhood in some way? Do your relationships reflect the same unhealthy patterns present in your parents' relationship? If so, you've likely identified a dominant negative emotion.

» Belief Probing: The keyword here is safety. If you met someone and fell in love, what would be the worst thing that could happen? How does being in a relationship feel unsafe?

» Morning Practice: Once again, you'll want to do daily positive aspects. Work on the way you feel about you. What do you love about yourself? What are your favourite parts of you?

» Other Exercises: Get specific. Do a sacred container to get clear about what that person you want looks like and how he or she makes you feel. Do focus wheels on why you'll attract that perfect someone. Complete a polarity processing exercise on polarities such as singleness versus being in a relationship, alone versus not alone, available versus taken.

#SHIFTCLUB

Ready to take action and get shifting? Log in to Shift Club and download the worksheet titled **The Relationship Breakthrough Worksheet**. *http://discoverthepowerofjoy.com/shiftclub*

Manifesting Purpose

Life purpose seems to be the third most requested desire when it comes to manifestation. Although it's not a physical desire such as money or a relationship, it's still important because without purpose, we often feel lost.

The first thing you need to realize if you're seeking your purpose in life is that nobody else can tell you what your purpose is. You can't calculate or compute your life purpose and the only one who truly knows your purpose is your inner being.

Why do we seek out our purpose? Because our ego likes to use it to identify who we are. We believe that if we can identify our purpose, we can then take a course of action that will make us feel more fulfilled. We often associate our life purpose with a career or a way to make money.

Have you ever considered that your life purpose may simply be to uplift others by being joyful? Or that your life purpose may be to experience joy and expansion in any given moment? Have you ever considered that your life purpose is to simply be happy and experience all the beauty life has to offer? To learn, grow, share, and experience?

If you knew what your life purpose was - assuming life purpose is a path or direction for you to take - what kind of void would this fill for you?

Try dropping the idea of needing to have a purpose. Your only purpose is to be happy. Are you afraid that without purpose you have no direction to point your sails? Your inner being is always guiding you down the exact path that will not only bring you fulfillment, but also bring you joy even if you can't see it. The simple step you need to take is to start following your excitement. Don't worry about if or how this purpose will bring you money. If you're truly passionate and excited about an endeavour, you're meant to follow it. Allow your inner being to take care of the rest.

Manifesting Purpose – Action Steps

» Seek Joy: If you feel stuck in manifesting your purpose it's because you're not tuning into the guidance being provided by your inner being. Drop the concept of purpose and focus once again purely on seeking joy. Seeking joy will help you reconnect with your inner being so that you can then gain the clarity and feel the excitement of where it wants to lead you.

» Emotional Probing: How does not having a purpose make you feel? Do any emotions surface when thinking of having a lack of purpose? Do you measure your own value in who you are or what you do? If you answer yes to any of these questions, you'll want to work on clearing these emotions.

» Belief Probing: What would be the worst part about identifying a purpose? In what way would having a purpose feel unsafe?

» Other Exercises: Polarity processing is a great way to flush out issues around your life purpose. Work on polarities such as knowing versus not knowing, having purpose versus lack of purpose, being useful versus being useless.

#SHIFTCLUB

Ready to take action and get shifting? Log in to Shift Club and download the worksheet titled **The Life Purpose Breakthrough Worksheet.** *http://discoverthepowerofjoy.com/shiftclub*

PART 3

The Principles for a Powerful Existence

PUTTING PRINCIPLES INTO PRACTICE

CALVIN, A MATURE STUDENT in a business program, contacted me in order to receive some coaching. In our first session, he discussed his biggest passion: filmmaking. Following close on the heels of filmmaking, his other top passions included rock climbing and spending time in nature. Calvin shared with me how at one point in his life he, along with a friend, had travelled the entire west coast of North America from Canada all the way to South America on a motorbike, documenting his experience through photography and film as he went. Although filmmaking was his passion, he was studying business. There was nothing he wanted more than to attend film school in New York so that he could make a living shooting film once completing business school. However, he had written off the possibility of a career in film due to the high cost of attending such an elite program.

A year after we had completed our work together, around the time of his graduation, a well-known Canadian outfitting company launched a nation-wide contest. Four winners would be selected to hike from one end of Canada to the other, and would be given camera equipment and camping gear to film the experience. Calvin, excited by this amazing opportunity, immediately got to work submitting a video entry, which he spent hours crafting, along with a Facebook page to support him in his attempt to win the contest.

A few weeks after the submission deadline, Calvin received a phone call. He had been selected, amongst thousands of entrants across Canada, as one of the top ten. His next step was to fly to Toronto for a weekend event with the other finalists where four winners would be chosen. News of his achievement quickly spread and he was even interviewed on the radio before flying to Toronto.

Calvin had a blast during the two days he spent in Toronto and things went amazingly well. He made great friends, was given free camping gear and other equipment, and gave an amazing presentation that blew away the judges and other contestants. To his surprise, however, Calvin wasn't chosen as one of the four winners.

Happy with his achievement but disappointed that he came so close without victory, Calvin returned home to put his focus back on his daily routine. Shortly after his return, he was once again in touch with the radio station that had interviewed him prior to departing for Toronto. They offered Calvin an opportunity to spend the summer visiting various nature-oriented tourist destinations. His job would be to film and photograph his experiences and host a weekly radio interview discussing each trip. Although the opportunity didn't pay much, he was excited about the chance to do the filmography, in nature, and excitedly accepted the position without hesitation.

As the summer wrapped up, and his radio work was coming to an end, Calvin received another phone call. It was a head-hunter from a company in another province who had seen the work he had published over the summer. They offered him a job, doing videography and spending time in nature which, needless to say, he quickly accepted. It was the exact work he was most passionate about, but he hadn't been able to see how it would be possible without attending film school.

From time to time, I spend moments reflecting on where I stand in my own life, and how I got here. I don't think I'll ever stop being amazed at the synchronicities that have taken place and the events that have aligned to get me to where I am today. At no point in my past could I ever have imagined myself living the life I am living and the surprising turn of events that has taken place. Even more amazing, as I look at how the last five years of my life have played out, it's as if I can almost see how it was all mapped out long before any of it took place.

If there is one thing that I've realized, it's that everything really is always working out for each and every one of us.

I can see with crystal clarity that I've been on a path my entire life. Each one of us is on a path and we're all being guided down the path that serves us best. Sometimes, we create a belief that a specific goal is unachievable because our conscious mind can't logically figure out the path to the desired destination. Our inner being, however, having such a broad view of our experience, is aware of all possible paths at all times. Not only is it aware of all the paths; it is constantly working on guiding you to your desired destination, utilizing the best possible option. If at any point you feel like you may have messed up the path your inner being has laid out for you, or taken a wrong turn on the road of life, there is no need to worry. Like a GPS, your inner being is always correcting your route so that you're always on the best possible path to your desire.

The more I've surrendered to my experience, the easier it has become to follow the path laid out in front of me. Surrendering has made me realize that sometimes what seems to be a failure may, in fact, be a blessing in disguise. When Calvin found himself as runner-up in the contest, it was initially perceived as a loss. Little did he know this was the best possible outcome. If he had won the competition he would have spent the summer travelling and would have missed the opportunity with the radio station. This meant he likely would not have been noticed by the company that ended up hiring him and the opportunity that ultimately led him to doing paid videography work - his lifelong dream.

It's taken me years of studying various concepts to help me build the trust to follow my path. To learn to listen and allow on a daily basis so that I can flow through live with the greatest amount of ease.

In the chapters that follow I share with you some of the most important concepts taught in spirituality and personal development. The concepts are the ones that most helped me along my path. When applied and put into practice, these concepts will help you in your daily life, especially when learning to work more closely with your inner being. They will help you expand the way you see and experience your reality and assist you in developing a greater sense of ease in your life.

YOU'VE GOT TO HAVE FAITH

ONE DAY, AS I looked back on the more difficult events in my life, I realized that each and every one of them brought me to a better place. Working in a volatile tech start-up industry, I was frequently let go as each company went under. Every time a business went under, I carried over the perfect tool belt of experience for my next employer. I was always hired at a better wage and accumulated bigger and bigger severance packages. Each business, like a stepping stone to the next, lead me to my final tech company which ended up being acquired for over 300 million dollars. This success allowed me to move away from the tech industry and follow my passion, working with others full-time as a breakthrough specialist. The same can be said for relationships. Each past relationship should not be seen as a failure, but as a stepping-stone to an even more rewarding, more loving relationship, tailor made to your exact preferences.

Each time the Wright brothers developed, tested, and subsequently crashed one of their prototype airplanes, they were one step closer to achieving flight. Every single design that didn't work was not a failure, but a step toward accomplishing their dream of creating a flying machine. In the same way, the seemingly failed experiences of your own life aren't actually failures, they are stepping-stones on the way to the greatest accomplishments in your life.

Looking back on your life, do you perceive the events that didn't turn out in your favour as failures or successes? In Calvin's story, finishing runner-up in the national contest was initially perceived as a failure. Yet, looking ahead to the opportunities that presented themselves because of this perceived failure easily shifts the perception to one of success.

Learning to trust in your experiences isn't always an easy task. Trust can't be ordered on Amazon or found by reading books (although it can help). The only way to develop genuine trust is through experience.

The day I pulled out behind the vehicle with the license plate "TRSTGOD," I had the biggest epiphany of my existence. If there was a force greater than me, who could subconsciously direct me to a specific place at that specific time in order to receive that important message, then who am I to doubt any of my experiences?

We are all guided. Not by an invisible force that judges us and our every decision, but by something so great, so powerful, and so loving, that it even allows us to decide if we want to receive its love or not. It always loves us, always cares for us, always co-conspires to assist us in living out our biggest dreams and desires. Unfortunately, most of us are unaware of this force or have disconnected ourselves from this unconditional love and the guidance it provides.

It took time for me to even build up my trust to a level where I could follow my intuition. It began with small synchronicities that served as constant reminders to allow my experience to be what it was and to detach from the outcome. The license plate was the event that changed everything for me. It's what allowed me to truly let go of the need to control and manipulate my experiences and instead allow myself to become a willing and eager participant in them.

Realize that when it comes to learning trust, your conscious mind never has the full picture; only your inner being does. Calvin's inner being perfectly arranged for him to be runner-up so that he could eventually land the job he always wanted. This was never a path Calvin could have planned for himself yet, he was in a place where he was able to follow his excitement and allow the universe to deliver his desire to him.

If you want to grow your faith and develop a stronger sense of trust in your experience and your inner being, the first step is to acknowledge that you don't know what's best. You have a limited viewpoint and not only do you not know best, you never know how a circumstance will play out and can benefit you. Trust will help you more easily flow through the difficult and unpleasant situations you will experience.

When difficult situations and unwanted circumstances surface in life, we have a tendency to push against them, bury them, or ignore the reality of the issues with the hope that they will go away. Sometimes, we fail to realize that these problems, although unpleasant, serve a very important purpose. They exist in order to help us grow and expand. They help to catapult us forward toward new understandings and new situations that serve us better in the end. Our conscious minds want to disallow these situations and label them as bad. The truth is that we don't know how these situations will play out or where these situations will lead.

When faced with adversity, we have two choices. We can choose to resist the situation and push against the current. Or, we can allow it, embrace it, process it, and flow through it with grace. Like a raft floating down a river with an unknown destination, we can choose to cling onto the rocks with the hope that it won't get any worse. Or, we can trust that the bumpy ride will eventually calm down and have faith that we are being led somewhere that will serve us better than any other point in the past.

The parable of the farmer and the horse is a great example as to why we shouldn't judge our experiences as good or bad. By simply trusting and allowing our experience to be what it is, we can hopefully find a greater level of inner peace.

The farmer and the horse

There once was an old farmer who had worked his fields for many years. One day, his horse ran away.

The farmer's neighbours expressed their concern.

"You are having such bad luck," they said.

"Maybe," replied the farmer.

The next day his horse returned accompanied by three beautiful, wild, horses.

"How wonderful!" the neighbours exclaimed.

"Maybe," replied the farmer.

The following day, the farmer's son decided to ride one of the wild horses. It threw him off and he broke his leg. Once again the farmer's neighbours visited him to offer their support and express their concern for his misfortune.

"You are having such bad luck," they said.

"Maybe," he said.

The next day, military officials arrived in the village to recruit young men for the army. Seeing that the farmer's son's leg was broken, they walked on by. Yet again the neighbours paid the farmer a visit, but this time congratulated him on how fortunate he had been.

"How wonderful," the neighbours exclaimed.

"Maybe," replied the farmer.

This story is meant to remind us that even though a situation may seem unfavourable, it could be, in fact, a blessing in disguise. We cannot control circumstances, but like the old farmer, we do have the ability to control our emotional responses to those circumstances.

Learning to trust is a skill that, like any other, is developed over time. The more you consciously decide to trust the more you realize that things are always working out for you.

FOCUS WISELY

Take a few moments and take note of the things you've placed your focus upon since you woke up today. Did you focus on things that feel good and uplift you, or have you been focusing on negative circumstances that bring you down?

When you decide to turn on your television, do you tune into a channel that entertains you and feels good, or one that's boring or makes you feel bad? There are many channels to choose from, but you can only select one station at a time.

Your reality is much like a television. At any given moment, you've got myriad circumstances playing out. Just as you would tune into a channel on the television, you get to choose which circumstance you want to tune into and focus upon. Will it be relationships, or how much money you have in your bank account, or work, or family members, or what you'll do this Friday night? Reflecting on some of these circumstances might make you feel good. Maybe you recently received a new promotion or a big raise. Other situations might make you feel bad. Perhaps a relationship with someone you loved recently ended or a good friend decided to move to another city. You can't always control the circumstances in your outer world and how they'll play out, but the one thing you can control is where you put your focus.

You only ever have one point of focus. Your life has multiple scenes all going on simultaneously, and like the director of a movie, you get to choose which one gets the spotlight. You have the power to choose to focus on those things that make you feel good or those that make you feel bad.

Do you watch the news? Do you focus on the negative aspects of the world such as war, famine, and suffering? Does giving these topics your attention uplift your emotional state? Or does it have the opposite effect and bring you down? In what ways do you believe putting your focus on these events serves you? By watching the news, filled with the unpleasant happenings in the world, are you helping solve these problems? Have you considered the impact it has on your vibration and therefore your attraction point?

Once you become aware of your own thought patterns and gain better control over your point of focus, you may begin to notice what the people around you are choosing to focus on. Since it's human nature to want to solve problems, we naturally put our focus on issues needing solutions. But, now that you've read a greater part of this book you realize that your circumstances are a reflection of the contents of your attraction point. By focusing on the circumstances that create negative emotions you're actually propagating the negative and attracting more of it. Focusing on the negative and worrying circumstances not only pulls you away from your state of joy, but also dampens your connection to your inner being.

When I realized the amount of time I was spending focused on the unwanted circumstances in my life, I changed my approach. I stopped giving them the same kind of attention. As a result, I started to feel better and experience more consistent levels of happiness, and noticed that my problems began to feel less severe. They also seemed to begin to resolve themselves of their own accord. I would wake up with sudden inspirations for new solutions. The synchronicities and higher guidance discussed in previous chapters became much more frequent. This doesn't mean that I don't deal with issues as they arise. The key, for me, is to address them from a good-feeling place, to let them go, and to move on, rather than trying to solve them from a place of angst or frustration.

My experience with focus made it easy to see the benefit of maintaining a higher state of joy. In giving more of my attention to those things that made me happy, my "Wi-Fi" connection to my inner being was stronger, and I was more prepared to receive the solutions it was providing to me.

I wasn't ignoring the problems in my life or pretending they weren't there. I acknowledged them and dealt with them. But I chose to limit the amount of focus I would give them to the absolute minimum. I patiently waited for the best solutions to present themselves to me. They always came when I felt good, and when they did I acted upon them.

It's not only the events in your life that you likely allow to dictate your emotional state. If you're like many people, you may allow the way you feel to be controlled by the people around you as well. When I'm giving talks or workshops, people often ask me how to prevent others - especially family members - from controlling them or the way they feel.

If a friend drops in for a visit how do you believe their emotional state will impact the way you feel? If they walk in smiling, laughing, cheerful it will most likely uplift your mood. On the contrary, if they walk in sad, upset, and angry there is a good chance it will pull you out of your happy place. When those around us are experiencing negative emotional states, it's easy to jump on board with their suffering or drama. Sympathizing with the struggles of others is not a problem. However, allowing ourselves to become sad, angry, or distraught with them does not help their situation. We don't help a sad person by choosing to be sad with them.

If the emotions of someone in your vicinity are at a more negative place than where you stand, what is your best course of action? Does dropping into a more negative state with them help uplift them to a happier place? Not only does this not serve them, but neither does it serve you. The best approach is to hold your ground, remain happy, and help them shift their focus. By doing so, chances are they'll feel better *and* be in a more receptive place to receive guidance from their inner being.

Remember that negative emotion reduces our connection to our inner being and it's that very connection that brings about flow, positive experiences, and ultimately the best solutions to our problems. The best way to help those struggling is to remain in your state of joy, which will also encourage them to join you. Be so happy that you inspire others to want to join you in that happy place as well.

Choosing your focus point will take some practice, however, over time, focusing solely on the positive will become second nature. In fact, the more you do it, the more you benefit from it and the easier it becomes. You always have the choice to decide through which lens you want to view the experiences of your reality. Do you want to view it through a lens of gratitude and positivity? Or, do you want to place your focus on negativity and circumstances that bring about negative emotions? You have the power to choose. You're the director of your point of focus and only you can decide where to put it.

THE POWER OF NOW

IF THERE IS ONE aspect that kids have nailed when it comes to knowing how to live life, it's their ability to be in the moment and live in the now.

My kids recently took a trip with their mom to see Disney on ice. Although I wasn't able to go with them, I could only imagine the number of "are we there yet?" moments and bathroom breaks during the five-hour drive. I like to videoconference with them as much as possible and was excited to receive a call from them during the Disney show intermission. My daughter was the most excited I'd ever seen her and probably spoke more words per minute than any other human in history. She was in sheer awe of all the magic that was surrounding her. Near the end of our conversation I asked her if we could FaceTime tomorrow, hoping she would fill me in on the rest of the show.

Her response?

"Daddy, we're FaceTiming right now!" she exclaimed. This was accompanied by a look of total confusion.

Although the concept of remaining in the now and being present in the current moment is simple, very few people spend much of their time there. Have you ever realized that most of your worries are rooted either in fears concerning the future or in events that occurred in the past?

How much fear, anxiety, or sadness do you believe you would experience in the moment if your memory was erased and you had no conceptual awareness of the future? Probably none. We often give up our emotional power to events that occurred in the past or events that haven't even happened yet, and might never even take place!

In this very moment, right now, every single event that has ever occurred has absolutely no impact on what you are experiencing in this second. Those past events are part of the journey that got you to where you are now, but unless you're continually focusing on them, they have no impact on the present moment.

Let me repeat it one more time.

The now is an end result of past experiences but is not being impacted by them (unless you allow it to be, by giving your attention to them, of course).

This relates back to your focus point. Those who suffer from chronic sadness may be suffering because of the negative momentum they create by continually focusing on unpleasant events and circumstances of the past. They just can't let it go. They are continually choosing to focus on memories that bring them sadness. If they could completely erase the memories of the past, and clear their inner inbox, would they still have a reason to be sad? If you want to live a joyful life from this day forward, does focusing on your lost puppy dog, or the failure of your business, serve you in the current moment? Do sad memories of the past prevent you from going outside, having fun, or spending time with friends? If so, it is only by continually dwelling on them that we allow them to do so.

The same goes with the events of the future. People with anxiety issues often suffer because they're focused on hypothetical situations created by the mind that, in this present moment, aren't (and may never be) real. Are you worried a meteor will come crashing down on your house or that the sun will suddenly implode? Likely not. Then why worry about other hypothetical circumstances that may never occur that are beyond your control? When an unwanted situation occurs you will handle it as best you can. Placing unnecessary focus on potential problems will not help you deal with those problems if they do in fact show up. As a matter of fact, focusing on the problems creates stress and negative emotions that may make you less resilient and less resourceful. Ironically, your focus on the problems actually increases the probability of attracting the circumstances you fear through your attraction point. In addition, your fears also keep you disconnected from your inner being, which is there to help you get the things you truly want.

You are most powerful when your focus resides here, in the now. Why bother giving anything else any attention?

When in the now, you're better suited to hear the guidance provided by your inner being. If you're busy worrying, thinking about the future, or staring at your phone while walking down the street, you may very likely miss an intuitive message to go into a specific shop or notice a friend walking by. When you are fully present in the current moment, your receiving channels are wide open.

Mind you, thinking about past or future events isn't always bad thing. If the possibility of an upcoming event excites you or if a past event makes your feel good, I encourage you to focus on these thoughts. By placing your focus on those things that make you feel good, past, present, or future, your attraction point will benefit as it helps you create more positive momentum.

LIFE IS LIKE A PUZZLE

BOTH OF MY KIDS are huge lovers of puzzles. Puzzles of flowers. Puzzles of dinosaurs. Puzzles of cartoon characters. It isn't uncommon for me to sit with them and do two or three puzzles in a morning. The joy of puzzles isn't in the final, fully assembled end product, but rather, in the time spent putting them together. If the fun was really in the end product, rather than the assembly process, we wouldn't pull it apart to put it back in its box so we can do it all again later.

The process of putting together a puzzle has a significant parallel to the way most people live life. When we are intent on achieving specific outcomes, our lives become more focused on the desired end result and not on the process of assembling the puzzle pieces. If we are focused on how happy we will be once the puzzle is assembled, we completely forget about the joy and fun, ready to be experienced, all along the way.

If I challenged you to experience joy for an entire day, where would you start? You would need to start by experiencing joy, for each hour, one hour at a time, for a twenty-four hour period.

How do you experience joy for a whole hour? By choosing to do so for sixty consecutive minutes, one minute at a time. How do you do that? By choosing joy for sixty consecutive seconds, one second at a time.

Right now, in this very second, you can't make yourself happy in a second that will occur later today or tomorrow. This moment has no control over the level of joy you will choose to experience in any other moment. You only have control over the second you are currently experiencing. You'll never create a lifetime of happiness by achieving a circumstance that will guarantee happy for the rest of your life. You create a lifetime of happiness by choosing to create an infinite number of tiny happy moments of which you only have control over right now, and right now, and right now.

Do you believe you're living life for the enjoyment of the journey or for the achievement of a destination? If you're finding yourself living life under the pretence of "I'll be happy when," then you're most likely living your life for the completion of the puzzle, rather than for the enjoyment of the puzzle itself.

YOU CAN'T OUTSOURCE HAPPINESS

THE PEOPLE CLOSEST TO you can be some of your greatest sources of joy and happiness. Lovers. Children. Brothers and sisters, parents, and friends. Spending time with those you love rightfully makes you feel good. We've gone into great detail about how your state of being, and the level of joy you experience, is up to you. You cannot depend on outside circumstances, including other people, to make you happy.

Those you love and care about, however, may not understand that.

What happens when the people around you put the pressure of their own joy and happiness on your shoulders? What happens when they set expectations, which, when unmet, put them into states of unhappiness, meanwhile putting the blame directly on you? Or what happens when they get upset at you for not visiting often enough? For not remembering to take out the trash or send them a birthday card? For not acknowledging the painting they just hung in the living room? For not wanting to go with them to the supermarket or join them at a social event?

What should you do when others blame you for the unwanted circumstances of their lives and for the way they feel? Well, you could buy them a copy of this book, however, a solution may not be that simple.

Sadly, this type of behaviour is far from uncommon. Many individuals find themselves in co-dependent relationships, giving their power away because in some way they feel responsible for the happiness of those around them. Some even feel unsafe if those around them are unhappy and they do everything they can to prevent that from happening. This may especially be the case for our family members, our partners, and our children. There is an added sense of responsibility that comes with family ties, an added sense of needing to fulfill the requests of another, because when they are unhappy, we allow ourselves to become unhappy as well.

What can you do about it?

Unfortunately, you can't control the behaviour or needs of someone else. No matter how hard you try or how badly you want those people to change, they are going to behave exactly how they choose to behave. Everyone does the best they can at their level of consciousness. Ultimately, they have a choice. They can choose to be miserable. They have the right to create a reality exactly the way they want to create it, regardless of how much pain or pleasure it brings them, or anyone else. Good or bad, they have the ability to choose to treat themselves and those around them (including you) in any way they please.

But you also have the right to choose how to respond to their behaviour. You have the power to choose how you allow yourself to be treated and whether you want to make yourself responsible for their happiness. The way you allow them to treat you, and the amount of abuse you allow yourself to take from that other person, is your decision. You choose how much power you give to someone else with regard to how you're going to allow them to make you feel.

What's the most loving way to act toward someone in your life who is unhappy and putting that kind of burden on your shoulders?

First, detach from the situations they find themselves in. Make sure you are not putting the responsibility for how they feel on yourself. Acknowledge you have no control over their state of being. Only they can control how they feel, not you. By trying to make them happy, you are actually doing them a disservice. You're preventing them from learning how to be happy on their own, and helping them to create a dependency on others for the joy they feel. You're allowing them to make joy conditional on circumstances relating to you.

Second, inspire them to feel better. Your remaining in a good-feeling place might help encourage them to want to make an effort to be happy too. You can't easily convince someone to make a change you know they need to make. Regardless of how much you might want them to change, the only thing that will encourage it is if, at a deeper level, they want the change themselves. The only way someone is going to make significant changes in their life is if, deep down, they really want it. How do you make them want it? Be so happy they have no other choice but to be inspired to want what it is you have. Lead by example. You can choose happiness, regardless of circumstances, or you can choose to suffer. They have the ability to make this same choice.

Third, choose to keep your distance if being around those individuals negatively impacts how you feel. Always surround yourself with people who help you grow, expand, and shine bright. Surrounding yourself with people who bring you down does not serve you. If you want to feel good and create positive circumstances in your life, it'll be much easier when surrounded by positive, good-feeling individuals.

TIMING IS EVERYTHING

My current relationship with Anik is one that feels surreal at times. Not only do we share incredible synchronicities, but we also think the same and compliment each other in every way possible. It feels like everything a relationship could ever be. Although I'm not a fan of labels, some would label this a "twin soul" relationship.

Just as incredible as the nature of our relationship, was the timing of it. If the two of us had met years or even months prior, a lasting relationship would not have likely developed. Our past experiences, including relationships and subsequent marriages, were necessary for our own personal development and inner growth. Our individual inner work is what not only prepared us for such an incredible relationship, but likely also ensured we attracted each other at the absolute most perfect time.

If you have a peach tree growing in a field near your home, when do you decide to harvest from it? If you walk up to the tree and grab the peaches before they are ripe, they will be too hard and won't be sweet. It doesn't matter how badly you want the peach, how often you stare at it, you cannot control when the peach will be ready, nor can you hurry the process. You don't know when the absolute most perfect time to pick the peach will be. Standing there, watching the peach ripen, will only create more impatience and suffering at the thought of wanting the peach now.

Trust that when it comes to those things you want, such as a relationship, the perfect mate will manifest at the most perfect time. Your inner being knows exactly when to best deliver a desire to you. Allow the gestation period to take its course. Allow the universe to do the work and for the process to unfold naturally. You don't want to meet that perfect partner or find that perfect job if you're not fully ready for it. Your inner being is the only one who is aware and trying to force the process will only cause discomfort. Trust in knowing that your desire will show up when it is ripe for the picking, when you can and will, enjoy it the most. Trust that those yet-to-be-manifested desires are on their way and relax into the knowing that they will show up at the perfect time.

ARE YOU READY FOR A NEW REALITY?

WHILE WRITING THIS BOOK I would often find myself reflecting on my past. Where I was, once upon a time, sitting in a cubicle. Falling in line and living my life the way I thought it was meant to be lived. Never had I imagined that I would not only break free from this mold, but that I would one day be helping others break free and realize their dreams as well.

Thanks to the guidance of my inner being, I've been on an amazing path that has led me to magical places, a path that has allowed me to witness and take part in some of the most beautiful experiences. A path where I know everything is always working out for me and where things just keep getting better and better. It's a path that is open and available to anyone who wants to hop on board.

In a previous chapter I asked: "Why this now?" Why am I writing this book now? Because it's in my flow and it excites me. Why do I believe my inner being is guiding me to write this book now? Because I feel people are ready to be empowered for more. I think it's time that we all stop ignoring our inner being and the guidance it provides. Because I believe that it's time to seek out happiness through our inner world rather than through our outer world. Because I believe people are ready to set themselves free from their emotional baggage, from their hindering beliefs, and to thrive.

What about you? "Why this now?"

Why is now the perfect time for this book to find you? Why did your inner being put this book on your path? Was it given to you by a friend, or family member, or did it find you in some incredible synchronicity? In what way is this book acting as a stepping-stone and where is your excitement guiding you next? Are you ready to follow it?

Where is your inner being guiding you next, and are you ready to listen to it and take action?

Your inner being is always supporting you through your growth, and I'm here to support you as well. Through my online program, my coaching, my Facebook page, and even email. Although I may not respond as promptly as your inner being can, I would love to hear about the shifts you make, the synchronicities you experience, and respond to any questions you may have.

It is my hope that this book has helped you awaken to new truths and an expanded awareness. Know you are never alone and are always loved. Your inner being is always present, guiding you, assisting you, and keeping you safe. The dreams you hold, old and new, are closer to reality than you might think. Your reality and circumstances are not to be feared. Your life is designed to be a joyful and expansive experience each and every day. The joy you seek and the experiences that accompany it are here for the taking.

Harness the power of joy and become the powerful co-creator you are meant to be.

CARE TO SHARE A LITTLE LOVE?

IF YOU ENJOYED READING *The Power of Joy*, and feel called to help me out, would you hop onto Amazon and leave a short review? Every single review counts and it would mean a lot to me.

You never know whom this book might help. It could be a friend struggling with inner peace or a co-worker who has never felt safe in a relationship. If you think others would benefit, please feel free to write a post on your Facebook wall or share a picture on Instagram (bonus points if the picture includes this book!). Don't forget to mark it as "public" and use the hashtag #thepowerofjoy; you never know what kind of prizes I might decide to give away to my followers. :)

I'm always just a click away and would love to connect with you. Find me on Facebook at http://facebook.com/nkbreau, on Twitter at http://twitter.com/nbreau, and Instagram at http://instagram.com/nkbreau. I love providing support in any way I can. In addition to my online support community at http://discoverthepowerofjoy.com/shiftclub, I'm looking forward to providing other free tools and resources to help you unleash the power of joy in your life.

Now, I invite you to go out, and experience The Power of Joy!

RESOURCES

Online Resources

The Power of Joy – Shift Club *(http://discoverthepower-ofjoy.com/shiftclub)*

Get instant access to powerful guided meditations to help create positive momentum during your morning practice or to clear negative emotions. Worksheets designed to help you apply the powerful processes in section 2. Instructional videos and guided tapping videos to help you learn EFT to shift negative emotions and beliefs. A book can only take you so far and this platform is designed to assist you in fully applying the formula I've taught you in this book. I've personally put this platform together and included everything you need to get results. If you're ready to change your life and do the work, I highly suggest joining my online community. Imagine what could life be like in just six weeks from now if you started applying these teachings today!

AAMET International (http://www.aamet.org/)

Association for the Advancement of Meridian Energy Techniques (AAMET) is currently the largest professional EFT association worldwide. If you want to become efficient at tapping or become a certified practitioner I highly recommend the AAMET programs. When working with an EFT practitioner make sure you are working with someone who has trained with or been certified with a credible organization.

Abraham-Hicks Publications (http://www.abraham-hicks.com/)

I'm always blown away by the number of workshops and events put on by Esther Hicks and the Abraham-Hicks team each and every year. These events range from half-day events to week-long cruises which take place all around the world. If you enjoyed the material in this book I highly suggest attending any Abraham-Hicks event that may be going on in your area.

Suggested Reading

Over the last decade I've worked with dozens of coaches and teachers, attended many workshops and seminars and read more books than I can count. I've decided to list below a subset of the books that have brought me the greatest amount of joy and transformation. Each of these books has been fundamental to the way I now live my life. Although my list is always evolving I've decided to post those most relevant to the teachings in this book. I highly recommend taking a look at each and every one of them if you haven't read them already.

Ask and It Is Given: Learning to Manifest Your Desires, by Esther Hicks and Jerry Hicks
The Law of Attraction: The Basics of the Teachings of Abraham, by Esther Hicks and Jerry Hicks

The Law of Attraction: The Basics of the Teachings of Abraham was the first book in the category of personal and spiritual development that I can remember reading. Although it was over ten years ago and I wasn't able to apply it at the time, I came back to it later in life and understood it in a very different way. The *Law of Attraction: The Basics of the Teachings of Abraham* and *Ask and It Is Given: Learning to Manifest Your Desires* are usually the first books I recommend to anyone asking for suggested readings. When working with my private clients I assign them homework with exercises based on some of the *Ask and It Is Given* processes.

The Power of Now: A Guide to Spiritual Enlightenment, by Eckhart Tolle
A New Earth: Awakening to Your Life's Purpose, by Eckhart Tolle

The Power of Now: A Guide to Spiritual Enlightenment and *A New Earth: Awakening to Your Life's Purpose* are probably two of the most talked about spiritual books of the last decade. I've found no other author has been able to dissect the concepts of the ego and living in the present moment better than Eckhart Tolle. I have read *The Power of Now: A Guide to Spiritual Enlightenment* a number of times and pick up new tidbits of knowledge with each read.

Think and Grow Rich, by Napoleon Hill

A classic in law of attraction circles, *Think and Grow Rich* by Napoleon Hill was originally published in 1937. By 2011, over 70 million copies had been sold worldwide. Jerry Hicks (of Abraham-Hicks) confided that the multi-million dollar business he created before meeting Esther Hicks was due entirely to a chance reading of *Think and Grow Rich*.

Spirit Junkie: A Radical Road to Self-Love and Miracles, by Gabrielle Bernstein

Another one of my favourite books for newcomers to the spiritual genre is *Spirit Junkie: A Radical Road to Self-Love and Miracles*. Gabrielle Bernstein shares her story of triumph over addiction. Following in the footsteps of Marianne Williamson, many of her teachings come from *A Course in Miracles*. This book is for anyone who enjoys storytelling mixed with amazing lessons.

The Tapping Solution: A Revolutionary System for Stress-Free Living, by Nick Ortner

Possibly the best selling book on EFT, Nick Ortner, with the help of Hay House Publishing, seems to have brought tapping to the mainstream with *The Tapping Solution: A Revolutionary System for Stress-Free Living*. While the best way to learn to tap is in person with certified instructors, this book is a great resource for anyone who wants to learn the basics of tapping.

Metaphysical Anatomy: Your Body is Talking, Are You Listening, by Evette Rose

Possibly the most used book in our home, *Metaphysical Anatomy: Your Body is Talking, Are You Listening?* by Evette Rose is the evolution of *Heal Your Body* by Louise Hay. With nearly 700 medical conditions listed, Evette provides multiple pages of emotional and belief root causes for those conditions, as well as key points to explore. I reference this book with all my clients and the accuracy of the information she provides is stunning. If you're interested in learning more about the possible inner root causes of anything from planter warts to cancer I suggest ordering a copy of this book.

Wishes Fulfilled: Mastering the Art of Manifesting, by Dr. Wayne W. Dyer

While I could easily list any book published by the late Wayne Dyer, *Wishes Fulfilled: Mastering the Art of Manifesting* is my favourite. Wayne has always been able to break down the concept of manifestation with a simplicity matched by no other author.

The Monk Who Sold His Ferrari, by Robin Sharma

Robin Sharma is another great storyteller who embeds valuable lessons in the storytelling of *The Monk Who Sold His Ferrari*. This is one of the first suggested readings for those who have busy careers and are looking for balance or purpose in their life.

51046998R00120

Made in the USA
San Bernardino, CA
11 July 2017